# Need You Now

## A STORY OF HOPE

BY  *plumb*

WITH SUSANNA FOTH AUGHTMON

SHOE PUBLISHING / STREET TALK MEDIA
NASHVILLE

**Shoe Publishing Inc. / Street Talk Media, LLC**

Nashville, Tennessee

FIRST EDITION PRINTED AUGUST 2014

Printed in the USA

Softcover:  ISBN:  978-0-9906172-0-4  |  UPC: 748252840851
Hardcover:  ISBN:  978-0-9906172-1-1  |  UPC: 748252840950
E-book:  ISBN:  978-0-9906172-2-8

10 9 8 7 6 5 4 3 2 1

*To the four most incredible reasons to believe there is always hope:*
*Jeremy, Solomon, Oliver, and Clementine.*
*I love you with all my heart.*
*Always, forever. No matter what.*
*More than all the dust on the moon.*

# Need You Now

*A Story of Hope*

# Contents

# Foreword

When I closed the last page of Tiffany's book, I wanted to applaud. Against the odds, in the wake of a fractured relationship that had lost all of its luster, hope appeared. Not in the epic stuff of modern storytelling, but in the simplest most profound way, like a seedling that springs up unexpectedly overnight, growing right out of the naked dark soil.

I texted Tiffany immediately.

"I just finished your book! I'm so glad that the gray Sunday afternoon scene in which I'm picturing you includes Solomon Fury, Oliver Canon, Clementine Fire, and Jeremy Lee."

Tiffany and Jeremy Lee had survived the relationship crash that inevitably happens, even on a straight road, when the steering wheel slips a little off center. Is it part of every couple's story that the romantic love that brings them together always falls prey to the weight of the burden of life? When the children we long for, the career goals we work toward, and the beautiful homes we dream of slowly become a reality, does everybody's life unravel?

Mine did.

So why am I, a divorced woman, writing the foreword to this book?

I'm writing it because hope looks different in each of our lives. Hope shows up when we stop hustling for what we think we want and what we think we need and who we think we are and let God have His way. Some of us have to crash and burn before we'll let go. When we finally do, though, we discover with fresh appreciation what God has been doing all along throughout our lives—providing unexpected serendipitous moments, directing us across the paths of people who are integral to our journey, and surprising us with experiences and opportunities that we are too timid to even imagine dreaming. This is the road to be on!

And the good news is . . . It's never too late.

**Amy Grant**
**2014**

# Preface

It is a rare thing to meet someone who is a kindred spirit. Someone who looks at life the same way you do, laughs at the same things, and values the same things. When Tiffany Lee and I met for the first time in the airport in Boise, Idaho, we already knew we had a connection. We had been admirers of each other's work and been friends online. We had texted funny things and encouragements to each other. We had prayed for each other. But when we decided to work together to write Tiffany's story, we knew we needed to spend real time together. A few texts weren't going to cut it. So I flew out to meet up with Tiffany on tour. Sometimes meeting face to face with a long distance friend can be awkward. Or sometimes it can be like you have always known each other and slip into a conversation that you feel like you started a hundred years ago.

We started talking the minute we met. We talked for a day and a night. Then we got on the tour bus for Winter Jam and talked some more. We laughed. We cried. We talked about marriage and kids and poop. (The last two go hand in hand as any mother can tell you.) We talked about joy and heartbreak and redemption. And we talked about the great hope that comes when we trust in the One who loves us most of all.

Tiffany is a rock star. I know this because I have seen her on stage and she has an amazing presence, her voice is incredible, and she wears much cooler shoes than I do. But mostly, Tiffany is Tiffany. She is real.

## Preface

She is authentic. She is honest. And she is, in a sense, every woman. She has hopes, dreams, passions, and trouble keeping her house clean. Just like me. Just like you.

And when we sat together, she told me about her awkward moments on stage (which I loved), her roller-coaster ride of a career, and the heartache and triumph of her marriage. It reminded me one more time that we, at our core, are the same. That we are all looking for hope and light and love and healing in the broken places in our lives.

And I think, as you read Tiffany's story, as you are drawn into her journey and root for her in the hard places and cry with her when she is hurt and let out a holler of joy when love comes through, you will realize, that you have also found a kindred spirit. And it doesn't get any better than that.

**Susanna Foth Aughtmon**
**2014**

# Introduction

Emily Dickinson has a poem that says . . .

*Hope is the thing with feathers*
*That perches in the soul*
*And sings the tune without the words*
*And never stops—at all.*

I think Emily knew what she was talking about. Hope. It's a word that fills something in us that moves us toward something better, something richer. It builds us up and urges us to share it. It's the thing that keeps us pushing forward even when it seems like the whole world is against us. And it never stops.

Some people find hope in the beauty that surrounds them. They see it in the pale orange light that hits the sky at sunrise with its promise of a new day, or in the first green of spring poking up through the snow saying that winter has ended. Others see it in the innocence of a newborn baby, curled up in her mother's arms. I love all of these things, but I tend to see hope in the darkest places and in the saddest stories. I think this is because that's where hope shines the brightest: Against the dark backdrop of fear and hurt and despair.

I have always been attracted to the dark. Not in a creepy, weird way, but in a that-can't-be all-there-is-to-this-story kind of way. If someone is sitting in the dark, I want to find a way to turn on the lights for them, and then, while we are at it, throw them a party. When I see someone who is sad, simply put, I want to make them happy. When someone is down, I want to figure out a way to make them laugh. I wanna crack open a jar of joy and see it light them up. I feel drawn to people who are struggling or hurting or lonely.

When I was little, my mom and dad sang in the choir and so they had to sit up on the stage during the service. My brother, who is three years older than me, would sit with his buddies, and my friends and I would sit together, giggling, passing notes . . . but eventually I always found my way to the sixth pew from the front where an elderly gentleman named Roscoe sat by himself every Sunday, silently taking in the service.

Roscoe was in his mid-eighties and a widower. He had an air of aloneness about him that I couldn't bear. He always sat at one end of the pew. I would sit at the other end. Just the two of us. We didn't talk but we were together. Desperately wanting him to know he was not alone, I silently willed him to find for himself the joy that I had inside me. I was hoping for him whether he knew it or not.

All it takes is one tiny moment of hope to lead to the next one and the next one and the next one, until finally you fall into an ocean of hope, so deep and so wide and so all-encompassing you can't figure out how you missed it in the first place. And you think to yourself, I couldn't even see this. I was so blinded by my fears and my hurt and my failures and my pride, that I couldn't see that there is this complete, massive ocean overflowing with hope. I know this because I have experienced it.

My life is just like the life of every human being who has ever walked this planet. It has good and bad and ugly and beautiful all mixed together. But in all of this lovely chaos that is my world, a single thread has woven itself through my life. From my happy childhood to my adolescent panic attacks, from my early Nashville years as a "newbie backup singer goes pro" to my sleep deprived moments of young motherhood . . . all the way to my marriage falling apart, a taut wire has strung the chapters of my life together like colored beads on a necklace. It has held me together when I was falling apart and lit up the dark on my loneliest nights.

Hope. It all comes back to hope. It's what strings the story of my life together: The story of dreams and family and love and Mr. Jeremy Lee. The story of IBS and depression and ADD. The story of written songs and three babies and a band and a shelved record. The story of an incredibly broken heart, a weathered storm, and a true, life-changing miracle.

Hope is the brightest word in the universe. It is the expectation that life, even though it's crazy or dark at the moment, can shift. That one tiny pinpoint of light can pierce the overwhelming sadness and break everything open with its joy. It's what we all want when we are hurting or full of doubt or heartbroken. We want some hope. I have a tank full of hope. I'm overflowing with it. Maybe it's because hope has saved me more than once. Maybe it's because it's saving me still. Hope is oxygen . . . and we all need to breathe. And my greatest wish for you, as you read my story, is that you will know this truth. No matter where you are, no matter who you are, no matter what you have done, no matter how dark your night, there is always hope.

# Chapter 1
## Hi, My Name is Tiffany

THERE IS NOTHING quite like standing on an outdoor stage with the summer sun beating down on you, singing your heart out, and feeling the crowd respond to you. Feet planted, heart pounding, everything you feel, everything you know, everything you care about is focused in the moment. You are connected.

Everything you were created to be is filling the air as you sing, pouring back out over the crowd. You see the expressions of emotion on the faces of the fans as they sing with you, fists in the air, shouting to the sky. Then there are those other faces, the ones with their eyes closed, arms raised, mouthing the words, as tears wet their cheeks. They are lost in the song. What an incredible raw moment to share.

In the best moments, you lose sense of the crowd altogether, and a song becomes a very personal, spiritual expression. You let go of your agenda, your ego, your worries about how flabby your upper arms look on the jumbotron, and your concerns about the weird echo in your ear monitors that happened during sound check.

It's not about you. It's about something so much bigger that you're simply a messenger. Singing center stage is no longer just a good show. It's a sacred moment. It's exhilarating. Intense. Beautiful. Heart wrenching. It's the very thing that makes everything you do worth it.

Sometimes you can't help yourself and you give into the moment. Climbing up on the drum riser, drenched in sweat, you catapult yourself into the air in an excited jump. You are one with the crowd. Your heart is racing. You kick your legs high. And in a heart-dropping moment, you feel your favorite vintage red velvet pants split wide open— and realize as the summer breeze wafts over you that you may or may not have decided to forgo undergarments with these particular pants since panty lines are not a good look on stage. There is that. In a space of six seconds, you are no longer one with the fans or a respected artist, you are just a girl with the wind blowing where your inseam should be. This can make it difficult to concentrate on singing or connecting or, well, anything really. Mostly, you just wish you could blink your eyes like a genie and be anywhere but where you are in that moment.

You get weird looks from your band as you finish the next *three songs* sitting with your legs crossed on the drum riser.

"She's still sitting!" their eyes are saying. "She's still sitting!"

But the show must go on, blown out pants or not. Finally, there is that humbling moment when you finish your set and realize that a respected fellow artist has seen everything, *everything* . . . and in his spontaneous kindness, he has brought a large towel to cover your shame so you can exit with a little dignity to the green room.

Life is like that: Joy. Amazing highs. Fantastic surprises. Unexpected moments. Embarrassment. Unbelievable lows. And blown-out pants all wrapped into one.

At least, my life is like that.

Hi, my name is Tiffany Lee, or as most of you know me, Plumb. I sing and write songs and have had more than my share of awkward moments on stage. I didn't plan on being a rock star . . . or a songwriter . . . or a performer. But the love of music and the joy of singing were woven into my DNA while I was still in the womb. It's who I am.

As long as I can remember, I have been singing. As I said, my parents both sang in the church choir while I was growing up. And although neither one of them would claim to be a great vocalist, Mom and Dad have always loved music and singing. My dad spent his days working different shifts for Delta Airlines, but he would wake us in the morning singing a made-up "Good Morning" song or one of the many little diddies he has been known to write while out on the lawnmower. A stay-at-home mom, my mom always referred to herself as a "domestic goddess." In our cozy house in Indianapolis, this Domestic Goddess was also a bona fide DJ. My mom washed dishes with Elvis on vinyl in the background. He shared the stage with the smooth sounds of Johnny Mathis and the raspy voice of Stevie Nicks. Every time I hear a Fleetwood Mac song, I am transported back to road trips in my mom's orange Chevette with the tan pleather interior. Windows down, curls whipping in the breeze, we belted out the songs together. I am convinced that the cassette player in that Chevette would only play Fleetwood Mac.

My older brother remembers those road trips less fondly. While quick to acknowledge my burgeoning talent, he considered me to be the musical thorn in his side. Even though I stayed over on my side of the line, or the "hump" as we called it, in the back seat of the Chevette, my vocal stylings did not. The sound of my voice filling the car and bouncing off the windows seemed to grate on his nerves. Or maybe it was the constancy of my singing. The fact that no matter where I was or what was going on, I was singing.

I just couldn't help myself. As I would sing along happily to whatever song was on the radio, he would beg my parents, "Please, p-l-e-a-s-e . . . make Tiffany stop singing."

I, personally, loved my singing. My parents, if anything, encouraged me. So my brother was left to his own devices when it came to trying to get me to stop. He was patient; I have to give him that. My absolute favorite toy as a child was our family tape recorder. I still have it. I loved to record myself. I entertained myself . . . with myself. I would record myself singing and then I would listen to the recording, rewind it, and tape over it with something else. I never saved anything;

I just liked to hear my recorded voice. (My best friend, Melis, will tell you that not much has changed in that regard.)

Anyway, one night my brother got a hold of the tape recorder, which he strategically placed just in time for dinner. In between passing the green beans and the fake instant mashed potatoes my mom always tried to convince us were just like real potatoes, my brother stretched his big ole' toe under the table and pushed, Play.

My voice erupted from below, yielding an awkward silence at our dinner table. My brother was triumphant. I was horrified. Those recordings were personal. Private. Not meant to be shared. I made a general disclaimer to the table, "I was just talking to myself." My parents were sympathetic. Brother got in trouble for embarrassing me. I ended the night triumphant.

Besides giving us a solid foundation of great music in our home, my parents gave us a solid foundation of Jesus. It isn't a stretch to see the marriage of those two things continuing on in my life even now. My passions for music and songwriting flow out of my passion for loving and following Jesus. I don't remember a time in my childhood when His presence wasn't felt or mentioned or referenced.

My dad came from a very strict, conservative Christian family. My mom came from a very loving and accepting non-Christian home. Our family was a mash-up of these views and traits. In our home, church life was central. Sunday was the Sabbath, the Lord's day, a day for Bible lessons, familiar hymns, and being with friends. Yes, I was raised with solid values, my mom's delicious fried chicken, and Jesus. If we weren't at home, you would usually find us at church or the thrift store. My mom and I love thrift stores.

I have an early memory of me standing on the stage of Southwest Church of the Nazarene in Indianapolis, Indiana. I am all of three years old. A microphone in my hands, I am dressed to kill in ruffles and tights with hair curling into ringlets about my face. I am singing a duet with my dad. I come up about mid-thigh on his polyester slacks. I am not afraid. I'm not nervous. I am happy. My mom sits in the congregation beaming; the infamous family recorder is on her lap taping my first live performance. My dad is beyond proud. Unbeknownst to me, he has told the soundman to cut his voice in the mains when it gets to the chorus, the part I know best. I can hear his strong baritone voice singing with me in the monitor, but all that the congregation hears come chorus time is my high warbling toddler notes as I belt out the words:

> *It reaches to the highest mountain*
> *It flows to the lowest valley*
> *The blood that gives me strength from day to day*
> *It will never lose its power.*

I still remember the powerful feelings of that moment, the swelling of the music in the sanctuary. The warmth and safety of my dad near me. The smiles on the faces of the people before us. Something big was taking place. This was joy. Plain and simple. The import wasn't lost on me, and I can recall that tiny girl thinking, I *really* like doing this.

J.D., an elderly man with lots of freckles and a big smile, approached me after the church service. Bending down so he could speak to me eye to eye, he said, "I hope you sing every Sunday. That made me so happy. That brought me so much joy." The truth of what he said showed in his face, the way it lit up and his eyes crinkled around the sides. And I believed him. I remember thinking that day that I wanted to make people feel like that for the rest of my life, whether it was singing or telling a joke, or giving a hug. In that moment, without realizing it, I found my thing. It wasn't necessarily singing. It wasn't necessarily being in front of a crowd. It was making people happy. I wanted to make people laugh. I wanted to give people joy. I wanted people to feel the way that J.D. felt.

I may not have understood the blood theology that I was singing about, the message that made J.D. so happy or that made my mom choke up that morning, but I knew that I liked Jesus and Jesus liked me. Knowing that was more than enough for me.

As for the understanding of all that Jesus had done, and would do, for me in my life, well, that would come later in a thousand different big and small ways. The foundation that my parents laid for me so carefully as a child became my anchor as an adult. As I have grown and changed, so has my relationship with Jesus and my understanding of who he is and how he loves me. He doesn't need me. He *wants* me. He doesn't need me to love him. He wants me to love him. No matter what I have done or not done. No matter how many mistakes I make or how many times I get it right or wrong. He just loves me. No matter what. It's just like I say to my children before I shut off the light at bedtime, "I love you. Always. Forever. No matter what. More than all the dust on the moon."

My relationship with Him is not about the dos and don'ts that I embraced as a child. It is simply about responding to His love for me in a way that never wavers. It is my bedrock. It is the thing that every other part of my life hinges upon: my music, my friendships, my marriage, my love for my children, and my parenting, but also the way I treat the cashier or the server or the person who hurts me. In Him is my true home, where my identity is found.

What my parents gave me, and what I found in church that day as a three-year-old, helped carve out a path for me to walk on as I grew up. What I wouldn't know for years is that a time would come in my life when everything I ever thought I knew to be true would be tested and shaken, leaving me clinging to the single truth I sang about that day as a tiny girl in ruffle butt tights: His power alone sustains me. His power alone gives me hope.

He would hold me at my highest peaks and sustain me in my lowest valleys. And He would ground me when things that were going very right, suddenly, went very wrong. Life at its best is unpredictable. In the years following the vintage red velvet pants catastrophe, I would find out just how unpredictable it could be.

# Chapter 2
## Joy is a Choice

GETTING TO LIVE out the dream of doing what I love—what I was born to do—is the best. Any musician will tell you the same. But living on a tour bus for several weeks straight or many months out of the year can be an adjustment.

A nice tour bus sleeps twelve people in four rows of three bunks each. This makes for close quarters. If you're not already close to your band members before you go on tour, you will definitely be close to them after spending week after week seeing them in what they call their "pajamas," eyes bloodshot from late nights, going through their unusual bedtime routines, or brandishing their distinct brand of "morning breath." You really do become a family.

After a late concert, everyone loads on the bus to wind down and wait. After tearing down from the night's event, the crew is packing equipment on the trailers behind the bus. Energy runs high, and, if you're lucky, warm bus food is waiting. Bus food is both fantastic and horrible all at the same time. Fantastic, because you are starving after a show. Horrible, because hot wings can be deadly at midnight. People chat, eat, laugh, and eventually slip off to their bunks. I always try to call dibs on a bottom bunk. Climbing into a top bunk requires you to get in your bed without stepping on someone's face as you use that person's bunk to launch yourself into your own.

Each bunk has its own heavy pleather privacy curtain so no one can see you drool on your pillow while sleeping. Once secure in your cubbyhole for the night, you have a little electrical station above your head to plug in your phone or tablet as well as a low light for nighttime reading. Sleeping on a tour bus can be fun. It's like summer camp on wheels. You and all your friends get to have a sleepover. Once tucked in you can say good night like the Waltons (we add nicknames on our bus), "Good night, Carp." "Good night, Jimmy Dog." "Good night, Giffy." "Good night, Tricky," and so on. Or you can simply put your headphones on, zone out, and surrender to the hum of the engine and its gentle vibrations rocking you to sleep like a soothing lullaby. It's cozy.

Unless someone closes your pleather curtain all the way, enclosing you in a space roughly the size of a casket. Then if you're me, you might panic a little. I need a good foot of open curtain space so that I can breathe in and out and feel the glow of the low light of the hallway on my face. I like to say that it helps me dream good dreams about the hot guy I'm married to and the cute little kids I get to see when the bus pulls into Nashville the next morning. No single thought brings me more joy than thinking about those sweet faces. Four unique kinds of joy: Jeremy Lee, Solomon, Oliver, and Clementine. My heart is full.

Life as a wife and mom on the road is an adventure, but I think I have always thought of life as an adventure. To me, joy and adventure go together. I have always been excited for the next fun thing, the next delicious treat, the next big gig, even the next year to arrive. As a preschooler, I once tried to convince my mom that I was four years old, through the door of the bathroom in our quaint little red brick ranch house.

"I'm four."

"No, you are three still."

"No, I'm four."

16

"No, you are three," my mother said, firmly.

"Well, I'm almost four."

There was a long pause on the other side of the door before Mom conceded, "Well, you are almost four, but make sure you always tell the truth, because you're actually still three."

I may have been only three years old to my mom, but in my mind I had already been there and done three. The day after I turned three, I considered myself almost four. Maybe it was because I was the baby in the family, or maybe I just got excited about what was coming next. Probably it was a little of both.

Being the baby in my family and the youngest granddaughter (one grandson younger than me on each side) definitely had its perks. My mom comes from a family of eight kids and my dad comes from a family of six. I have scads of older cousins. Every family reunion, every holiday, every gathering is something to anticipate because even in my childish heart I recognized that my relatives are always excited to see me. They grounded me in their love. They made me feel special. It is that eternal gift for which every child, every person longs. How can you not see life as a fun adventure, how can you not sense joy everywhere you go, when you are surrounded by people who love you?

My Great Uncle Rueben always called me, "The Boss." When I would walk in the door, his eyes would light up and he would announce, "Well, here's the Boss." There was something about me that was contagious to him. And there was something about him that was contagious to me. He couldn't get enough of me and I couldn't get enough of him, or his gigantic pillow belly.

Tucking my small hand in his calloused palm, we would walk out behind his house to the cornfield. Slipping between the rows, we would fill a basket with ears of sun-warmed corn. His wife, my Great Aunt Mae, would let me help shuck the corn, and then she would boil it in a large silver pot. The cobs would drop into the scalding water firm and come out sweet and soft. We ate them dripping with butter. They tasted like candy.

I remember thinking, This is the good stuff. Shucking sweet corn.

A house full of cousins. Hugs and kisses from my aunt and uncle. This is it! I would leave their home feeling rich and full.

My mom once took me aside when I was older and, with an arm around my shoulders, said, "Don't take it lightly that you bring joy to people. I almost named you 'Joy' because I just liked the name. Sometimes I wonder if that's what I should have named you. You bring joy to others; don't ever stop doing that."

She was probably being a little dramatic because she almost named me Monica, too, but she was right: I was a joyful kid. Maybe she breathed prayers of joy over me while I was in her belly. Maybe she just encouraged it in me along the way. Wherever it came from, if I could find a way to give anyone around me some of that joy I carried inside, I would. It was what motivated me in church, in school, and with my family. It motivated me in my friendships, too.

One of my best friends in elementary school came from a broken home. It wasn't something we ever talked much about; it just was. She lived with her mom. She didn't know her dad. And I couldn't stand it. I felt like if there was some way I could tuck her into the folds of my family, I could fill up the hole that had to be in her heart. I wanted her to have what I had. I wanted her to feel the safety, the wholeness, the sense of stability that I had. I had my full share of joy and I wanted her to have her full share, too.

But in recent years, I have learned a few things about joy. It isn't something you can hand off to someone else. It exists independent of whether you have one parent at home or two. And it isn't happiness. Happiness is circumstantial. Happiness is that feel good emotion we all love. A lot of things make me happy: Root beer. Coconut. Chocolate. Black Licorice. Coffee. Hot herbal tea. Massages. Shoes. Romantic comedies. And good old-fashioned fart jokes, to name just a few.

Happiness, at best, is a quick fix. It is a momentary pleasure. It always has a beginning and an end. It's not that I don't love being happy. I adore it. I would love to be happy every single minute of every single day for the rest of my life, but I have found in my long lonely nights when one simple spark of happiness cannot be found, joy is still there.

Joy can light a path in the dark. It can weave its way into a broken heart and strengthen a weary spirit. Joy and hope are best friends. They are hand-holding friends. You can't have one without the other.

This is because joy is not an emotion. Joy is a choice.

Joy is not simply a response to something fun or life-giving or exciting. It is an attitude that we can embrace whether life is easy or hard. Good or bad. Funny or tragic. I love how Kay Warren puts it in her book *Choose Joy: Because Happiness Isn't Enough.* She says, Joy is the settled assurance that God is in control of all the details of my life, the quiet confidence that ultimately everything is going to be all right, and the determined choice to praise God in every situation. Hope is something that is birthed out of joy. If I truly believe that God is in control of the details of my life, if I really understand that ultimately everything is going to be all right, and if I choose to praise God in every situation, a space opens up in my soul that allows me to dream, to pray, to hope. I have joy, so therefore I can hope. Once you have hope, the sky is the limit.

I could have used Kay Warren's kind of joy in junior high school. Junior high has a way of sucking joy out of the most resilient of children. When I was eight, we moved to Fayetteville, Georgia. My dad was transferred by Delta, and we were very settled into the community by the time seventh grade hit. But somewhere in the mash-up of changing classes, lockers, premenstrual hormonal upheaval, and the sheer terror of dressing down for PE, my sense of calm and my love-filled childhood gave way to paralyzing anxiety, anxiety that would lay me out flat and leave me gasping for breath, desperate for hope like never before. It crowded out the easy peace and security that had filled my early years. And it didn't leave a lot of room for hope. Every time a panic attack hit, it squeezed out, literally, any thought of hope. I felt as if I were going to die. And joy, well, joy flew out the window.

# Chapter 3
## Potty Talk & Panic Attacks

THERE IS ONLY ONE rule on the tour bus when you are on the road. That rule is this: Rule No. 1, no number two. In other words, no pooping on the bus. That may seem like a weird rule, but it is one that everyone follows religiously. The bus has a working toilet, but the delicate inner workings of the bus's sanitation system doesn't welcome solids. And no one wants that system to go down— that's for sure.

For most people this is no big deal. But for one Tiffany Lee, it is. That rule makes me anxious. I want to know that if I need to poop, I can. Driving through the night out in the middle of nowhere, bathrooms, even nasty gas station bathrooms, can be hard to come by. And not being able to use the one nearby toilet makes me anxious and more likely to need one. Why? Chalk it up to the diagnosis of one gastro doctor (after a series of privacy invasions) as IBS, or Irritable Bowel Syndrome, which can often make potty time a painful time for me.

I spend so much of my time in the bathroom, finding the humor in it is a way to deal with it, I guess. It's not that I have an affinity for bathrooms, but that I have always been a little on the crude side. I won't lie. Gross things make me laugh. When I was little, my dad would scrunch up his mouth as small as he could, stick out his tongue, and talk in a funny voice, calling himself, Billy. Billy always talked about poop. I thought my dad was bring-down-the-house hilarious when he talked like Billy. But Billy didn't come out to play very often. Both my dad and my brother were pretty selective about what gross things they thought were funny. I had no such reservations. Gas? Funny. Burping? Funny. Potty talk? Funny. If there were a line to be crossed, I could be counted on to cross it. At which point my dad would say to me, "Tiffany, why do you always have to take it to the gutter?" I don't know Dad, maybe because the gutter is funnier.

Since becoming a mom, I have taken on the role of Billy in our house. I can scrunch up my lips and talk about poop like nobody's business. My kids adore it. They have my comical sensibility. Jeremy, however, can't look at me when I do it. My becoming Billy takes some of the romance out of the day as far as he is concerned.

I think my affinity for gutter humor and potty talk, my love for accessible bathrooms, and my anxiety at not being able to locate one when I need it, comes from the fact that by the age of thirteen I had developed panic attacks from the IBS. Little wonder given that it manifested itself in gut-wrenching lower abdominal cramps and a crippling social fear of being without a bathroom when I needed one. After all, what are a few jokes about gas when you have experienced an upper GI, lower GI, barium enema, colonoscopy, and unending laparoscopic procedures? Nothing was sacred. My private parts were all but public. The only way to get through it was to laugh. And of course, pray.

The first time one of my paralyzing attacks took place, I remember going into our downstairs half-bath and having the worst stomachache I'd ever had in my life. I screamed out to my mom for help. I could hear the fear in my mom's voice as she threw open the bathroom door. "Tiffany, what's wrong?"

I tried to explain the cramping, the excruciating tightening in my belly. The pain was so intense I couldn't think. I couldn't talk. Mom was as scared as I was. She didn't know if it was my appendix or a horrible case of the stomach flu.

At that moment, I felt like I was dying. I could barely breathe, and I felt that if I couldn't get some kind of relief fast, I might lose my mind. Trying to go to the bathroom didn't help. Lying down didn't help. Standing up didn't help. The pain had me curled in a fetal position, clutching my stomach, tears streaming down my face.

I didn't know what was happening to me. I didn't know that every day for the next six years, I would experience one of these attacks. Sometimes they were brief; sometimes they were long; sometimes multiple attacks occurred in a day.

That day at home with my mom began an endless round of doctor visits that would pepper my days for years to come as they tried to decode what was going on in my gut. Internists. GI docs. Endocrinologists. Gynecologists. Each one weighed in with theories and medical treatments. They wanted to rule out the obvious: Constipation. Krohn's disease. Endometriosis. Ovarian cysts. Colon cancer. They put me on record levels of fiber. I was taking muscle relaxants like M&Ms, trying to calm the cramping. The little blue pills provided some relief at home but weren't so great for school. The problem was that by Spanish class, not only was my lower intestine relaxed but also my brain, and my eyes were crossing. The condition affected my schoolwork, my emotional state, and my social life.

We started calling the daily attacks "my stomachaches." But at one point, one of the doctors took my mom aside with a question of his own: "Mrs. Arbuckle, do you think that Tiffany is a hypochondriac? We're just not finding anything medically wrong with her."

My mom answered, "I can assure you she is not a hypochondriac. She has missed out on doing the things she loves because of them. She gets horribly embarrassed when she gets sick in front of someone. She isn't faking. This is real."

And it was real. It was a nightmarish kind of real. The kind of real that you just want to escape from. I didn't want to die, but caught up in the mind-numbing agony of one of my stomachaches, I wasn't sure

I wanted to live either. I wanted out of the pain and the humiliation and the crippling fear. Each paralyzing bellyache fed the fear that had started to grow in me: The fear of getting stuck somewhere in pain and not being able to make it home, the fear of never knowing when a new stomachache would come but knowing with a dreaded certainty that it would come, the fear that this would be my story for the rest of my life.

I didn't want to go to summer camp unless my mom was the chaperone. I didn't want to go on the youth mission trips unless my parents were going. I didn't want to go out on dates outside of a ten-minute radius of my home. This did not bode well for romance, although dating remained a favorite pastime.

When I look back on this time in my life and try to understand how a happy little girl who had never experienced a moment's worry became a teenager plagued by debilitating panic attacks, I think of the year I turned thirteen. Hormones were kicking in, and my childhood was receding into the distance. I went from a stable elementary school environment to the high-energy peer pressure of junior high. Managing locker combinations, mastering training bras, and "going together" with boys proved to be a trifecta of emotional upheaval for my world.

The fact that any of us survive junior high with our psyches intact amazes me. The mind/body/spirit connection is so strong. I had no idea at the time that the pain in my colon was directly connected to my nervous system. But I knew that the only thing that seemed to penetrate the pain was the knowledge that I was not alone in my fear.

As the years passed, I developed a routine for when one of my stomachaches would come on. I needed a toilet, a warm bath, a heating pad, and the comforting hope that comes from prayer and scripture. I recited Isaiah 41:10 like a mantra. More than one day at high school, I hunkered down in stall number four in the bathroom of Building D, tears gathering in my eyes as I whispered, "Fear not, for I am with you; be not dismayed, for I am your God. I will strengthen you. Yes, I will help you. I will uphold you with My righteous right hand."

Repeat. "Fear not, for I am with you; be not dismayed, for I am your God. I will strengthen you. Yes, I will help you. I will uphold you with My righteous right hand." Repeat. "Fear not, for I am with you; be not dismayed, for I am your God. I will strengthen you. Yes, I will help you. I will uphold you with My righteous right hand."

The prophet's truth wore a path in my soul.

God promised that He was with me—that He wouldn't leave me and He wouldn't give me more than I could handle. I took Him at his word. I added Psalm 46:10 to my arsenal: "Be still, and know that I am God;"

And then Lamentations 3:22-23, "Through the Lord's mercies we are not consumed, because His compassions fail not. They are new every morning; Great is Your faithfulness."

Doctors couldn't fix me, so prayer became my only safety net. God was always there; even in my difficulty I was still breathing in and out. God started to replace my fears with hope. It took years of different medications and altering my diet and a growing confidence in my Creator to make me less anxious. Slowly I developed more endurance, enough to make it through the next panic attack.

You would think that panic attacks would make it impossible for me to travel and perform. That the sheer act of standing up in front of thousands would bring my entire digestive system to a screeching halt. But God has a way of surprising us with His faithfulness. He is never put off by our weaknesses or our shortcomings. I have learned that when we have to fully lean into Him that we become more than we could ever be on our own.

In junior high I would never have guessed that the path that was being laid before me would involve traveling and performing before crowds of people—and a tour bus that I couldn't poop on.

# Chapter 4
## Paying My Dues

PREPARING AN ARENA for a full-scale concert is a major undertaking. When the tour bus arrives at the venue after driving through the night, there is already a crew of men hired by the arena prepping for its arrival. Multiple artists and buses only amps up the craziness of set up.

The sun has barely lit the sky when most of the buses roll past security into the back lots and loading docks of the arena. As soon as our bus pulls in, carefully organized chaos begins. The setup crew moves with a kind of frantic precision—each person and each task depends on the other to get the work done. It's a little like watching the construction of a skyscraper on a time-lapse video. You can't believe all the moving parts required at any given time.

Scaffolding, stage construction, lighting, and sound all have to be carefully coordinated. While giant monitors and various other gear are being wheeled up ramps and secured in place, huge bins of merchandise for each artist are being transported to the concourse to be set up and sold. Catering has arrived, and breakfast is hot and ready for those arriving. Dressing rooms are sourced and showers are located. Tour managers check in with the production office that coordinates everything from sound checks to security detail to backstage passes. Each person involved in the tour has a certain task to perform in order for the event to work. As it is, each day is not without its challenges. There are always a few hitches. That is life on the road. Or maybe I should just say, that is life. Each night is a mini-miracle when the lights actually come up and the musicians hit their marks.

In just a few short hours, thousands of eager listeners will fill the arena. The pressure and excitement mounts as the clock nears the time of the opening set. In the wings, different artists are giving interviews. Radio and TV personalities ask probing questions about the personal side of the musicians, with follow ups about their life and music—the articles and TV segments that follow will impact ticket sales. For the artists getting ready to perform, it can be a surreal experience. Most of us didn't start out singing in front of twenty people let alone twenty thousand. We don't take standing on stage and sharing our hearts for granted. It is a gift. It takes more than a walk up the ramp to get on stage. For some of us, that walk has taken years.

Every musician starts somewhere: a high school garage band, talent show competitions, coffee houses, county fairs, or dive bars. But when I was growing up, while I did perform at such places, I preferred to sing in nursing homes and homeless shelters. I got a lot of love from the geriatric and homeless communities.

My mom was a part of a small weekly Bible study that I sang for on occasion. The third Thursday of every month her group would combine with other small groups in the area for a larger meeting, and she would use me as the special music. As I said, she was a bit of a DJ and a bouncer. You should have seen her push those elderly fans off me when they got too crazy. After hearing me sing, ladies would ask my mom, "Would your daughter come and sing at our church?" or "Would she sing in our coffee shop?" Little by little my name was passed around for different events. By the time I was in high school, I was singing outside of church at least once a month.

I had my own karaoke machine and microphone and an assortment of background tracks. I also borrowed songs from a collection of tracks from our church choir room. The music minister let me borrow them for my singing gigs as long as I returned them afterwards. I had a full range of songs from Susan Ashton and Cindy Morgan to Margaret Becker and Out of the Grey. I didn't know how to get access to Top 40 song tracks so I had a full-blown gospel set that I sang to instead. The day that I came across "Wind Beneath My Wings" by Bette Midler was a special day. It became a big one in my repertoire, my make-them-weep-in-their-seat-song. I could fly higher than an eagle when I was singing that song.

I came into the fullness of my singing glory one Saturday morning at the request of a dinky AM radio station in Atlanta. I was asked to sing at the local roller-skating rink. The rink had no special lighting or sound techs, just the flashing lights of a disco ball, the clickety-clack of countless rental skates, and the lovely scent of nacho cheese and stale popcorn in the air. I took my karaoke machine and stood on a little carpeted platform off to the side of the rink. This area was usually reserved for out-of-control skaters who needed a safe space to slow down and regain control.

My mom was with me that day, and the humor of the situation was not lost on her. She was snorting, she was laughing so hard. I was more than a little offended. My face was a deep shade of red. It was all so humiliating.

"I'm not laughing at you," my mom told me. "I just feel like one day this story will be told, and it'll be a good one. This is what we call eating humble pie."

"Mom, please stop talking," I said. "This is so embarrassing. Let's just do this and get out of here ASAP."

My one hope was that the skaters would be so focused on learning how to skate backwards they wouldn't notice much else, much less make eye contact with me. I plugged in my karaoke machine, as the skaters flew past me. You need a loud sound system and a good rendition of "YMCA" to really get your groove on while skating. My little karaoke machine did not have the necessary volume to compete. There was very little "rocking out" going on as I sang at the top of my lungs, "Fly . . . fly . . . fly away." But I powered through—for a whole half-hour I powered through.

When I finished my set, my mom's face was set in a permanent grin. I kept my head up just long enough for the station manager to hand me a coffee mug with the station's logo plastered on the side, a fitting consolation prize for my complete and thorough humiliation. It was also my payment. My mom was still laughing as we found our car and drove away.

When I got home, I scrawled in Sharpie across the bottom of the mug "Most Embarrassing Moment Ever," and promptly threw it in the trash. My mom fished it out. She still has that mug. She still drinks her coffee out of it. She says that she prays for God to keep me humble when she sips her morning coffee out of it. She has what I call the red phone to God—a direct line—too direct sometimes. Given my steady supply of awkward moments on stage, my mom's prayers remain only too effective.

My journey as a singer was not without its rejections. I tried out for a traveling teen choir with my church denomination and my school choir, and didn't make either one. But being passed over didn't devastate me. I'm more of an, "Oh, well!" kind of girl. I have never been super competitive. For me, singing was about the joy of the moment. If they didn't want me then, oh well, I was going to keep singing anyway. I have found that the gifts that God has given us need to be grown. I think you start out with a little. And you have to be faithful with a little. I was never consciously trying to be faithful with a little. I was just having a good time. And I think God knew that.

He does know us better than we know ourselves. He knew I needed some time with the old folks singing hymns. He knew that I needed to carry a karaoke machine with me to my gigs. He knew that I needed a mom who believed in me but who also kept me grounded. He knew I needed a coffee mug as a lifelong reminder that I am who I am because of who He is and what He's given me. My journey into the world of music happened in His timing, not because I was grasping at something or trying to make something of myself. He opened and shut the doors in my life that needed to be opened and shut.

One Sunday when I was singing a solo in church, my youth pastor's wife, Marlene, happened to have family visiting. Her brother, Dave, and his wife, who were from Nashville, had visited our church several times over the years. Dave's brother-in-law had also been the youth pastor at our church at one time. After Dave heard me sing that morning he sought out his sister.

"You know, I heard Tiffany sing when she was younger, and now that I'm hearing her again, I think she's got real talent," he said.

"Well, we think Tiffany has a really pretty voice, too," Marlene said. "I'll tell her you said that."

"Well, I just want you to know that she's a star. You need to keep your eye on her," Dave said.

Marlene didn't say anything to me that day about being a star, but she pulled me aside later and said, "My brother, Dave, lives in Nashville and he's a songwriter. He thinks that you have a really good voice."

"Tell him I said, Thank you," I replied.

I didn't give it a second thought. But apparently Dave did.

By the time I was sixteen, Dave had approached me with an idea. "What would you think about coming to Nashville and recording some original songs written by me and my friends? Most of them have never been cut by anybody else. It would give you something to give out whenever you go sing somewhere. You would have your own CD."

I thought it sounded it like fun. Mom and Dad also loved the idea. It was definitely a step up from singing karaoke at the local roller-skating rink.

Dave chose the studio, chose the musicians, and chose the songs. He said he saw something in me. He invested in me with his expertise and his time. I will always be grateful for that. My dad backed up his belief in me by funding the project with money from my college fund. It was a different era in music. Nothing was digital and everything was to tape. The players we hired were A-list players with A-list rates. The entire process was exciting, like a musical Disneyland. I remember sitting behind the console as they were tracking the music. Something was growing within me.

That was my introduction to Nashville. I was like a kid in a candy store. I had no idea what the process of making a record was, but that week with Dave and his buddies was a defining moment of who I would become. Just as the stage is set for a giant concert and all of the moving pieces have to fall into place for them to work, God was orchestrating one more piece to fall into place in the puzzle of my life. I was fittingly clueless. I was singing karaoke. But He is never clueless. He was shaping my life, molding my preferences, introducing people into my life that would change my dreams and propel me into the design He had for me. Things were starting to get good. And there were no coffee mugs involved.

# Chapter 5
## Finding My Inner Backup Singer

I LOVE ESSENTIAL OILS. I have a diffuser going on the bus at all times. The healing aroma of wild orange, clove, eucalyptus, cinnamon, and rosemary filling the room are soothing and bring me a sense of comfort. They also bring a little touch of home to our home on wheels. They're good for us, too, as they pump antioxidants into this tiny enclosed space in which we are all forced to breath each other's air. Living in such tight quarters, you need all the good smells and germ-killers that you can get to stay healthy.

On the road, my band becomes my family. When my real family is along with me, my road family and my real family mesh together into one giant family.

This may explain why I am inherently picky about the people I choose to work with. Ours is not just a working relationship that revolves around musicianship. This is all about how we look at life and how easy you are to be around if we have to live within an arm's length of each other. This is about whether or not you think my can't-sit-still husband, Jeremy, is funny, if you get along with my manager Chris, and how adorable you find my children. Because my kids *are* adorable, and if you don't think that they are adorable than you are a weirdo and I can't work with you.

I have no need or desire to be surrounded by Yes men and women, but I do require people who are authentic, who challenge me, who love life and good music, and who are something of an expert at telling a good joke. And yes, I require people who love my kids. My producer's wife, Karin, once told me that the best way to love her was to love her kids. Then I had kids and realized how true that is. If you really, truly love me, you love my kids.

There is something about chasing a dream together in close quarters that forms an impenetrable sort of friendship in cement. The love birthed out of such an environment is organic, a very real blend of laughter and mutual admiration. We have all seen each other at our best and our worst. The bus is a great equalizer, one of those places where grace needs to abound. It has to for us to all get along. We get on each other's nerves at times, but mostly we look out for each other. We love each other. And, we remind each other to lock the door to the bus lounge when we are changing clothes back there because we really don't want to see each other naked.

My first time out on the road traveling with a band, I was not with my own band. It was a door of opportunity that cracked open the year after I graduated from high school. A friend I had grown up with was instrumental in bringing the opportunity about. His wife was a backup singer in Benjamin Gaither's rock band, Benjamin. The other backup singer had quit, and they were stuck playing a show in Georgia without an alto. Racking their brains for someone they could get to come sing on a moment's notice, my friend told his wife, "Well, this girl I grew up with lives in Georgia, and I think she's actually taking singing pretty seriously right now. She just made her own CD."

I was still living in Georgia after I graduated from high school. I was still wavering on where I wanted to go to college, though there was a Nazarene college that I had my eye on. The summer before classes would begin, I landed a job as a teller at a bank thanks to my mom's friend, Shirley, and started to spread my young adult wings. I loved interacting with the customers at the bank, loved that I was making my own money, and loved that the assistant bank manager was cute. All in all, a great first job. I had saved enough money to buy my own car, was paying my own bills, and enjoying the thrill of becoming independent. Life was good. And then it got better.

I was at the bank when the call came in for me. "Hi, Tiffany! You don't know me but my name is Benjy Gaither," said the voice on the other end of the phone.

I think I responded with something sophisticated like, "Who?"

"Your friend's wife sings in my band, Benjamin," Benjy continued. "We are short an alto for our show in Georgia and were wondering if you would like to fill in."

I knew Benjy's father was Bill Gaither, the famous gospel singer, but I didn't know that Benjy had his own band. And it was a little surreal to be called at work like that. Most singers don't get gigs while they are reconciling bank deposits. But I knew that my parents would be thrilled. And, like I said, I am always down for an adventure.

It took me all of two seconds to say, "Sure!" Because, why not?

Luckily, the cute assistant manager gave me the weekend off. Benjy sent me the songs and I memorized the alto part. The night of the concert went flawlessly. Singing on stage, melding my voice with the other backup singer and Benjy, came easily to me. Having sung in front of so many different people before, I wasn't nervous. No panic attack or stomach cramps. I had fun. And Benjy and his bandmates must have seen something in me, because at the end of the show, Benjy asked, "Hey, we have another show in Texas next week. Would you want to join us again?"

I did want to. I loved the easiness of singing with the group. After a few weeks of concerts Benjy asked, "Well, what if you just kept doing this?" It seemed like a natural fit. I don't like to orchestrate. I don't like to control my surroundings so that everything works out the way that I want it to. When I do, it always seems to turn out wrong. I try to be faithful with each opportunity. I've always felt like I had a sense for when God is providing me with one. And when that happens, I simply try to appreciate every little thing about that opportunity. I soak up the moment and I pour the best of who I am into it. Whether it was working at the bank or supporting Benjy with my vocals, I wanted to give it my best. I think that God gives us opportunities to use the abilities that He has given us. I wanted to use the talents that He had given me and I wanted to do it well.

Over the course of the next eighteen months, a time came when I realized I couldn't be both an excellent bank teller and an excellent singer. I needed to make a choice. I was working at the bank during the week and driving or flying to the concerts on the weekends. Neither was getting my full attention.

I loved the structure and steady income of the bank job, but I felt like it pulled me away from my growing creative side, the part of me that loved to engage people and spread joy. At the heart of things, I still had that same motivation that I had had as a child to put a smile on someone's face. Singing my heart out, hitting the notes, and feeling the joy well up in me was irresistible.

Even though I was just singing backup, I didn't mind being in the background at all. Sharing in the experience on stage was enough for me. Connecting with the audience, experiencing the way music has of touching souls and giving people hope, gave me what I needed. I couldn't get away from that. A new kind of world was opening up for me. That sense of togetherness that comes with sharing life with people who are passionate about what you are passionate about was starting to take hold of me. I wanted in. I was hooked.

I gave my notice at the bank and moved in with Bill and Gloria Gaither briefly in Alexandria, Indiana, until a roommate could be found. My parents let me go with their blessing. It was like my mom had died and gone to gospel heaven. Her daughter was under the supervision of Gloria Gaither for goodness' sake. It doesn't get much closer to Jesus than that.

The Gaithers generously opened their home to me, but I knew if I was going to follow the path of singing for a living, I would need to learn to be on my own sooner rather than later. I didn't just want to spread my wings; I wanted to fly. I was ready. Even though I would miss my family, I would soon find out that a new family of friends and artists were waiting for me just around the corner. And I could hardly wait. Music City, here I come!

# Chapter 6

## Apartment Living & Nashville Dreams

ONE OF THE THINGS I MISS the most when I am on the road is my people. My tribe. Nashville is home to the best folks in the world. My husband. My kids. My family. My friends. My church.

When I am away, I miss the way that Jeremy challenges me. The way he always has something new and exciting going on to share with me. I miss my kids and how they fill up my day with their wildness and their funny sayings. I miss getting to snuggle with them and kiss their sweet faces and toes and read stories before I tuck them into bed. I miss my friends. I miss the camaraderie and connections of living out daily life together. I wouldn't trade the opportunities that God has given me for anything—even if it does take me out on the road away from all this—but I have found my tribe is what keeps me real.

Touring can tend to be me-centered. What do I need to do to take care of myself? Where am I performing next? When is my next interview? What am I going to wear? What I am going to say in between songs? How can I improve my next set? How can I connect better with my listeners? How can I interact better with the guys in the band on stage? I am constantly thinking about myself. Not in an overtly selfish way, I hope, but more in a career-type way.

When it comes to the business side of being an artist, I am not just me, Tiffany Lee, wife, mother, doting aunt, and friend. I am Plumb, singer, songwriter, and performer. I have obligations and responsibilities to fulfill, like any worker has. At the same time, I strive for balance. I make a conscious decision not to become completely self-involved—despite the fact that such is the nature of this business. Promoting one's self. Creating a brand. Portraying a certain image. Moving to the next level. That's what artists do in Nashville, if they want to keep doing what they love.

At times the most well-intentioned of us needs someone to keep our ego in check. I have an entire clan of people who do that for me.

Jeremy and I have a group of friends that we have known for many years: Melis. Tara. Dodge. Ricky. Megan. Bryan. Chris. Brent. Daveta. Tammy. These people were present when we started dating. Most were at my twenty-fifth birthday party that Jeremy threw for me. A few of them were hiding out in the bushes filming and taking pictures when Jeremy proposed to me. They were in our wedding party. They have been in the waiting room of every baby's delivery and at every birthday party for each of our children. And we have done the same for them.

We love each other and cry with each other. And when one of us is sick or moving or has a new baby, we bring each other meals, because that is what real friends do. We are each other's best cheerleaders.

With these people, I am not Plumb. I am me. I am Tiffany. This is community. This is real life: Authentic. Messy. Busy. Full. Chaotic. Fun. Wild. Real.

Their love and their truth anchor me to reality. These people could care less that I sing. I remember my friend, Tara, also known as my maid of honor, standing off to the side of one of my first Plumb concerts when someone asked for my autograph. She started laughing. She looked at me and said, "I've seen you half naked, stirring a pot of Split Pea Soup. Why do they want your autograph?" I laughed with her. She reminded me, "This is not who you are. It's a part of who you are now, but who you are is the friend that I met singing backup and doing demos for free. That girl is still in there and that girl needs to stay in there. You don't ever need to forget who that girl is."

That is the kind of truth-telling that keeps me honest and real. They knew me in my pea soup days. Before the return address on my bills read Nashville, TN, I was already becoming friends with Tara and fellow roomy, Tammy. Before I even left home, God was already giving me the kind of friends that I would need to thrive in the years ahead.

Nashville wasn't a completely new town to me when I drove my Honda up the interstate to Tennessee. Besides making my little independent CD, I had been there with my church and visited the Grand Ole Opry with my parents. In a way it felt like coming home to something new. It felt familiar and unknown all at the same time. All of the band members from Benjamin lived in Nashville except for Benjy and the other backup singer. The rest of us would come in town on occasion. Tammy, the band's road manager who ran the tour, and Tara, the soundman's girlfriend, were both thinking about making Nashville their home. Tammy and the band's producer, Bryan, were getting serious, and Tara wanted a new start. As for me, I wanted to be around the energy of a bigger city.

I had lived with the Gaithers and with Tammy at her Aunt Moe's and with my brother as his roommate for months, but this next step was big. As I drove into the parking lot of Bent Tree Apartments, in Antioch, Tennessee, on August 14, 1995, it felt like my life was starting. I was growing up. I was twenty years old. I had with me all the new bedroom furniture and décor I had bought myself in the last year. And I had saved enough to buy a sofa, because everyone needs a sofa. And life with good friends and a new sofa was bright and shiny and wide open.

Tammy and Tara were the best first roommates ever. We all liked each other. They both had long dark brown hair and beautiful brown eyes; otherwise they were polar opposites. Tara needed sunscreen. Tammy, in the stark of winter, looked like a Cherokee because of the blood running through her veins. Tara was an Ann Taylor-loving preppy with khakis and a penny in her loafers, while Tammy lived in cutoff jeans and K-swiss tennis shoes or a bathing suit and was a total tomboy.

I landed somewhere in the middle. Tammy and I would go without makeup on for days, but I would borrow Tara's clothes when I wanted to look like a grown-up. Tammy would be gone before any of us woke up, destined to spend every waking second with Bryan. Tara was up at the first beep of her alarm clock, making one of her five allotted bagels for the week that she had so responsibly budgeted out. Then there was me. I would smell breakfast cooking but it wouldn't quite get me out of bed. I would sleep in until I absolutely had to be wherever it is I had to be. I had, at this point, started collecting jobs.

I collected jobs wherever I could find them. Not only was I singing backup for Benjy, but when Benjamin began touring with Lisa Bevill, another Christian artist, Lisa asked if both of his backup singers would sing backup with her, too. My name was passed around as someone who sang demos and backup. Nashville is a small community. If you have worked well with one artist, they will recommend you to their friends. I began getting calls to sing backup and sing in different studios on various records. I would show up for bus calls and sing backup for artists on various tours or sing for artists who were singing locally. Little by little, singing began paying my bills. I would make fifty dollars here or a hundred dollars there. I was also a babysitting fiend and practically a nanny for one child I absolutely adored. I also took a part-time job teaching gymnastics. And if money got really tight, I sold my clothes to consignment. And believe me, it got tight.

When I came home at night, Tammy, Tara, and I would hang out. We had people over to play games and watch movies and stayed up late talking. "The girls," I called them. Along with Tara and Tammy and I, that included Dawn, Bethany, Cathy, Kim, Karin, Rachel, Leslie, and Nicole. We would laugh and talk shop. We were caught up together in a place of hope. We were expecting good things to come out of this life. We were living the dream. We were rich in friends and fun. And as far as I can tell, that is the best kind of rich you can be. I've always been very content with my life. I don't have a deep well of longing in me that can't be filled. I'm not entirely sure where that comes from, but I've always had the feeling, Hey, if this works out, awesome! And if it doesn't, there'll be something different that could be equally as exciting. Still I was going to enjoy every minute of this while it was happening.

Even when I was teaching gymnastics to three- and four-year-olds who too often forgot to use the restroom before climbing up on the balance beam, I still had this sense that I was exactly where I was supposed to be, handling wet leotards notwithstanding.

In fact, standing behind someone else on stage and being a part of making him or her sound *really* good felt *really* good. Memorizing the lyrics to someone's new song and popping into the studio to record the alto line was truly fun. Helping out a fellow artist I had looked up to by watching their kids so they could take a phone interview made me feel like I was doing something valuable and building relationships.

My life was like a color-by-numbers at this point. There were all of these different areas being shaded in. Each of these jobs and tasks were shaping the picture of my life and who I was becoming. The fast friendship with Tammy and Tara shaped me. Our girlish hearts were headed toward becoming strong and capable women. The doors that kept opening for me kept reinforcing the love I had for sharing my voice. The odd jobs I was taking kept me grounded and reminded me what I was in Nashville for and what I wanted to do with my life.

Because at this point, I knew I wanted to work doing something I loved. I had no idea that the picture of my life was about to become bigger and brighter and more than I had ever imagined it could be. My life was coming into focus. And I couldn't wait to see what was going to happen next.

# Chapter 7
## Dreams Do Come True

EVEN BEFORE THE TOUR BUS pulls into the parking lot in Nashville, my mind is moving on to the things that I need to do when I get back home: Grocery shopping, recording in the studio, checking in with the kids' teachers, and talking with Jeremy about the house.

Our little house we have lived in for the last couple of years is set on almost five acres of lush green and wooded land facing a sweet little pond. It's my hope house, the house God literally gave us when we lost our big house. We bought this house when we were left dusty and bruised by life, but still believed that there was more before us than there was behind us. It isn't a spectacularly beautiful house to look at but it is safe and solid. I've learned that safe and solid looks spectacularly beautiful to the soul.

So I love this house. It is a house of healing and a house of new starts. Now that we are two years out from purchase, we are ready to remodel it to give us a little more space to stretch. As our kids are getting bigger the house is feeling smaller. When we had the contractor come and look at it, he said, "You know, with all the changes you want to make, it makes the most sense to just build up, instead of out . . . taking the roof off and allowing this to virtually be made into a new home."

And it seems that life is offering more than that. If you had told me two years ago that Jeremy and I would be talking about remodeling or building a new house together, I would have laughed, and cried—like Sarah did when the angel told her that at ninety years of age she was going to birth her dream baby. She couldn't help but laugh. That angel was talking about the impossible, but then again, that is how God works. We dream these little dreams that we clutch so tightly with both hands, and He says, Nope. That dream is too small. Think bigger. He dreams bigger. He dreams better. He dreams the dreams for us that we can't dream for ourselves.

I learned this early on after moving to Nashville. I came home one day after being out on the road with a new friend in tow. Adam was a bass player who played for a different artist we happened to be touring with. We had come back to the apartment to have lunch together when I hit the button on my answering machine.

A few calls came in each week from producers asking me to sing on their projects. I would get the information as to where the studio was and what time I needed to be there. When I showed up ready to record, they would play the song, and I would do my thing. Sometimes I was recording a demo in which I sang lead for the whole song. Other times, I would sing backup. I was the "oohs" and "ahs" in the harmonies. I have an ear for harmony so I could hear what I wanted to sing while listening to the song.

"Can I just sing it through a few times of how I'm hearing it?" I would ask the producer. "If that's completely off from what you're wanting, then you can direct me otherwise."

Sometimes the producer would say to me, "We have a very specific thing that we want to do with this song. We want you to sing this, this, and this."

I learned to be flexible. I also always wanted to be prepared to say, Well, here. Let me try this. Hearing different parts of a song in my head came naturally to me; it was like muscle memory. The more I worked at listening for harmonies, the easier it became. And it was fun. And as I said, I really like fun.

When I heard the machine beep that day, I just assumed it was another demo job, but the message said, "Hi, this is Robert Beeson from Essential Records calling for Tiffany Arbuckle. Give us a call." And he left a number.

"Essential Records is the record company that signed Jars of Clay," Adam said.

Jars of Clay had just come out with its huge hit, "Flood," that was getting airplay both on Christian and Top 40 radio stations. I thought, Great, and went back to eating my sandwich.

It was January 1996 when Robert Beeson left that message. I assumed I was going to get some work with Jars of Clay. Maybe the band needed a backup singer for its next project. When I showed up to the meeting, Robert had a different idea all together.

He was the artists and repertoire guy for Essential Records. An A&R guy scouts talent, signs talent, and develops how he wants that talent to be marketed to the world. The best A&R guys have a vision for the artists they sign. Much to my surprise, Robert wasn't interested in me singing backup or doing a demo. He was interested in me as an artist. Essential Records had heard me sing on the Benjamin CD that Benjy had just put out. The CD featured a duet with Benjy and an unknown girl singer, and they wanted to know who the girl was. The girl was me.

Essential Records was a new label. Jars of Clay was technically the only group it had signed at the time, but Essential was looking for its next artist. As I sat across the table from Robert, he explained what he wanted. He was a young guy, excited about how things were changing in the Christian music industry.

"I heard your voice, and I have been thinking that I would love to do something along the lines of a female duo, like ABBA or Ace of Bass. I really like your voice. I'm wondering if you would be interested in exploring something like that?"

43

I was more or less stunned (probably more than less). Before I could respond, Robert said, "I know you sing with another backup singer, would she be an option?"

"Yes!"

"So, why don't you talk to her, see if she's interested in something like that. I want to begin working on the record within the year."

I left the meeting thinking, What just happened? Is this for real? Someone wanted to sign me as a part of a girl band. Unbelievable. By the time I stepped outside, I was grinning and shaking my head. And thinking, this is crazy but crazy in a good way. I called my parents. I told my friends. We were all excited. It was one of those Disneyland dreams-do-come-true stories.

Some artists spend their whole lives knocking on doors, sending out demos, and singing in bars just trying to get a foot in the door. I had had a label come to me. I talked to my friend, Beth, who sang with me in Benjamin but she ultimately wasn't interested. She was newly married, and she and her husband agreed that they needed to focus on other things. My heart deflated a little but I understood. When I called Robert with the news, he didn't even hesitate.

"Well, do you have any other friends that sing that you'd be interested in pairing up with?"

My heart inflated again. There was still hope.

Sometimes, however, things are not meant to be. You would think anyone would jump at the chance to get a record deal and do anything to make it happen. Not so. Either my friends were involved in other projects or newly married or didn't want to make the commitment at the time. As quickly as my hopes had risen, they fell. This just wasn't working out. And I wasn't interested in being paired with just any ole singer off of the streets. I had worked in the business long enough to know that to work a duo or group requires a unique chemistry between its members, a true melding of minds and hearts. I believed it would take a unique friendship to make the music I wanted to make.

I met with Robert again. I can remember sitting across from him and breaking the news: "Just, never mind. Thanks, but . . . no thanks."

His eyes widened in what I could only surmise was shock. I tried to explain how I had got here.

"I haven't really found anybody in the time frame that you've given me," I said, "and I don't want to force something that isn't meant to be. Unless you're open to waiting until I can find the right person that's interested in the project, I'm not really interested in doing it."

I could tell I had surprised him again. "I really am so grateful to be offered this opportunity," I said, "but I don't really know how comfortable I am with you going and finding a girl and putting us together. It seems a little too Spice Girls."

Robert was silent for a moment. "So, you're turning this down then?"

"Well, yes, I am." My heart was pounding. I was nervous but I wasn't panicked. "I don't think this will work for me. Maybe two other girls will come up."

He was quiet for a minute. Well, there goes my shot, I thought. But I knew who I was and I knew who I wasn't, and I felt some relief at just being able to say, Sorry, this isn't me.

"Well, what if I just signed you?" Robert asked.

"Well, that wouldn't be the girl duo that you have in your mind at all," I said, not understanding.

"Yeah, okay, let's just forget that for a second," Robert said. "What if this meeting is not by accident, and maybe we're just supposed to work together?"

"Well, then I would definitely be interested." My heart was pounding in my chest again. "But I haven't even really thought about what I would be if I was a solo artist. What would I be?"

Then I began to answer my own question saying, "I definitely wouldn't be southern gospel. Even though I respect gospel, that's not my style. I want to be something that's real, that's not made up or forced."

"Well, what kind of music do you listen to?" Robert asked.

"I love The Cure. I love Alanis Morissette." I named a few more artists I liked.

"Have you heard of the new band Garbage? You should most definitely check them out," Robert said. "The band is female fronted and certainly not southern gospel . . . it's a mesh of what it sounds like you love, sounds like something you'd like."

So I did what he suggested, and I did like it. I loved it. And a more clear direction was found.

Robert told me later, "That moment you said you were turning down the offer connected with me. It was a game changer. You were so willing to try something that you had not even considered, but when it started to move in a direction that could be a little removed from who you felt like you were, you were completely fine walking away. I felt in that moment, this is someone worth taking a risk on."

I knew none of this at the time, but there it was. The dream that I had never dreamed was coming true before my eyes. It was a God dream. Bigger, better, fuller, more immense than anything I could have ever dreamed for myself.

I was going to be an artist: Not just a studio singer or a demo singer or one half of a duo but a bonafide-have-my-own-record-with-my-own-style artist. Essential Records signed me. For me. Tiffany Arbuckle, an artist in my own right.

I could barely breathe. It was too much. And it was all stretching out in front of me like a long wide road of hope.

# Chapter 8

## Picking Plumb

I HAVE A THING WITH names. I gravitate towards names that mean something. I probably get that from my mom. My mom named me Tiffany after one of her and my grandmother's favorite movies, *Breakfast at Tiffany's*. As a result, I am a diehard fan of Audrey Hepburn. I love everything about her. I think being named after such a classic beautiful movie influenced how I feel about myself.

Names aren't just names. They have a weight to them. They frame how you see yourself. Jeremy and I were very intentional about naming our three children. We love the different aspects of their personalities that their names reflect: Solomon Fury Lee, Oliver Canon Lee, and Clementine Fire Lee.

My dad and father-in-law were less than sure about Solomon's middle name. They weren't sure we knew what we were doing. They thought of "fury" in terms of anger and violence, but I had read the meaning of the word and knew it meant "intensely inspired; exultation; passionate." So now his grandpas love his name. Funny how things like that work out. More than once I have overheard one of them proudly saying, "Have you heard his middle name? It's Fury!" Solomon in the Bible was wise, a songwriter, and the son of David. My husband is the son of David Lee. I'm a writer. And my sweet Solomon is most certainly wise. I call him my wise old soul. I am eager to see all God uses him to do.

Solomon also means peace in Hebrew and Oliver means peace in Latin. I love that these two brothers are named peace, if only for all the times peace is the exact opposite of what these two boys are thinking about. It is a reminder to them in those moments of who they are.

Oliver is also a family name, and his middle name Canon also evokes a sense of power. We named him Canon, as in the law of scripture. And of all of my children, he is the one who tends to keep me on my toes with his curiosity and his daredevil attitude. Hiding God's word in his heart might be one of the most important sources of strength for our Mr. Adventure rock star.

For our daughter, we settled on Clementine, which means merciful. Her tender, compassionate heart makes the helpful caregiver in her very evident. I wouldn't be the least bit surprised if she finds herself working with those in some way less fortunate. Fire refers to refinement and purification; both processes that produce beauty and strength. I see those attributes in her on a daily basis. And then there is the fact that she is pretty much a firecracker. She may take after her mother in that way. Okay, in a lot of ways.

I love the strong powerful middle names we gave our children. The names are words that have been around for centuries, but they are unique and strong. It wasn't that we wanted them to have a name that no one had ever heard of before. We weren't making up some weird name like Smorgerfloffer that they would have to live down for the rest of their lives and try to explain away. Jeremy and I wanted to give them names with a sense of purpose. Solid names that would give them a solid foundation to grow and build on. Unique names that set them apart and build them up all at the same time.

I guess I was looking for the same type of name when I was searching for a name for myself and my band after I signed with Essential

Records. From the get-go, Robert had let me know, "Your first name is the same name as the Eighties' pop star, so FYI, we can't use your real first name." I was completely on board with that. I didn't want to use my real name as a stage name. I liked bands with names like Garbage and 10,000 Maniacs. Yet how do you pick a name that is going to represent who you are and who you hope to become? How do you pick a name that will reflect how you see life *and* that you will still like fifteen years from now? (God willing that people will still want to listen to you fifteen years from now.) The name-picking process was mind-boggling, a lot like how the record-signing process was mind-boggling.

Me, I was pretty clueless. I found a lawyer in the yellow pages to review my contract with me. My lawyer sat down with me and explained the legalese in the contract. Most of it made sense when he laid it out for me.

"The only piece of business that we have left to deal with is that they want you to sign off on your publishing. They want to own your catalog."

I laughed, "I don't even know what that means."

"All your songs that you've written," he explained, they comprise your catalog.

I laughed again and said, "I haven't written any songs."

He smiled again and said, "Well, they want to own them."

"Okay, well, they can own them." I thought it was funny. Years later, it would not be as funny, but in the moment, I was more than willing to give the record company the rights to all the millions of songs I had never written—after all 1996 was the year that my dreams were coming true.

Later, as we sat in the boardroom of Brentwood Benson Records, the parent label to Essential Records, where I was ultimately signed, across the table from the CEO, I felt like I was experiencing an otherworldly moment. I was all of twenty-one years old, and here I was at this watershed moment. This was the day the course of my life changed and my path became clearer. My parents were there to witness it, beaming with joy. A notary was there to keep everything on the up and up and legal. My yellow-pages lawyer was by my side. As the CEO slid a check for the recording contract across the table, he gave me a smile and asked a question.

"Can you sing?"

I smiled back and said, "Um, yeah."

Everyone chuckled. And then he slid another check across to me for the publishing portion of the contract and asked another question.

"Can you song write?"

I paused and thought about saying, No? The air was still. I had never really written any songs before but there was a sense of excitement pulsing through me. I cleared my throat and said, "I'll try!"

Everyone laughed. The meeting broke up. I hugged my parents, and shook hands all around, and took a quick photograph to document the moment. This was it. This was my big day. The dream I had never dreamed was happening.

In the weeks and months following that big day, I learned a lot about life. Sometimes things aren't quite what they seem. I had ten thousand dollars after my signing, which seemed like a fortune to me—until I paid off my lawyer, the taxes, and my one credit card. Then I had twenty-eight dollars. Still, I was debt free and an artist and living the adventure of a lifetime.

Essential was anxious to get me in the studio. It was July, and the label wanted me recording by December. I was anxious to get in there, too. There was just the one question, Who was I as an artist? I assumed Essential would be fielding songs from writers and handpicking the ones that would help to shape my sound and style. I thought the record executives would be finding songs that I loved, that I believed in, for me to pour myself into. Instead I heard maybe one or two songs pitched to me. Nothing that sounded like what I would choose to sing.

"Why aren't we hearing more songs?" I asked Robert.

"Well, we don't even really know what songs to have pitched to us because we're not even sure what the sound is yet," he reminded me.

The excitement of being signed was coupled with the confusion and frustration of knowing that I was supposed to be recording soon but I had nothing to record. I may not have known a lot about the music business, but I knew that it's difficult to make a record without any songs.

"Well, I've given you some examples of what it is I think I would want to do. I definitely want a style that's edgy, that addresses hard subjects, but that also conveys a message of hope at the same time," I reminded Robert. It might not have sounded that mature but that's the jist of what I was trying to tell him.

Eventually, it became more and more clear that any songs that I wanted to sing with an edgy message of authenticity and hope would have to be written by me. Shaped by me. Me, the girl who had signed away the rights to her publishing catalog but who had no publishing catalog to draw from for her first record. The irony was not lost on me.

I think I have mentioned a time or seventy that God dreams things for us that we wouldn't even think of dreaming for ourselves. Essential was taking a chance on me. I had to prove myself. And Essential had to prove itself as a new label. It didn't have endless amounts of money. In a way, we were both winging it. Some people may think Essential was using me to its advantage, but I look back and see God as using all this to His advantage. I was being forced to write songs. And in that process God was revealing Himself to me. And He was showing me who I was going to become. I can't imagine not writing my own songs now. Writing is as much a part of me as breathing.

Once, when we had been talking about styles of music that I liked, Robert mentioned a new album to me by an artist I was already fond of, "You should check out Suzanne Vega's new record, *Nine Objects of Desire*."

An amazing songwriter, Suzanne is very pointed and poetic at the same time in her songs. She uses metaphor to reveal her vulnerability in a way that is unique to her. One afternoon, pondering the fate of my not-yet music career and my not-yet named band and my not-yet recorded record, I was listening to her song, "My Favorite Plum."

I loved her up close and intimate, breathy voice, as well as the sharp lyrics. I thought I'd put the CD on repeat but had put the *song* on repeat, and so I found myself hearing the word "plum" over and over. Plum. Plum. Plum.

In the warm still air of that summer afternoon, my name found me. Plum. When I presented the idea to Robert, my neighbor Matt Bronleewe, who would turn out to be much more than that one day, was with me.

"How would you spell it?" Matt asked. "Plumb with a 'b' or no 'b'? If you add a 'b' to the end it won't mean the fruit . . . but so much more . . . it'll mean 'true.' "

Plumb. True. Yes, that is exactly what I meant. Plumb with a "b." Plumb. It was me. I was it. I had found the perfect name. Now I just had to write the songs that fit the name. I was excited and scared all at the same time. But mostly, I was ready.

# Chapter 9

## The Poet in Me

RECORDING STUDIOS ARE some of my favorite places in the world. Some of my most creative, mind-stretching moments have taken place in writing sessions there. Whenever I am in Nashville, I tend to be in the studio—whether it is working on a song for an upcoming album or collaborating on someone else's album.

I am a writer at heart. Since childhood I have been attracted to words and how they flow together. I could have read Shel Silverstein's *Where the Sidewalk Ends* once a day. The way he plays with words inspires me.

Hours upon hours have been spent with a legal pad in hand, or an open laptop illuminating the table around me, as I search the heavens for words to encapsulate what I feel about life. That is really what my songwriting is about. How I see life and how it has shaped me. What I love and hate about it. My music truly is a reflection of my life.

There is a sense of joy that comes from forming words and notes into something that resembles part of your soul. I tend to write from extremes, be it my own experiences or from the experiences of people that I love or met for a moment. Some of my songs have an aspect of darkness to them, and they talk about the heartache that we encounter in this life. I try to craft some of my songs into little pieces of light that reflect the goodness and joy I've experienced. Like when I write about how my children make me feel or about the all-encompassing love I have for Jeremy Lee. Both types of songs are pictures of hope set to music. It's the way that I connect with humanity. Let's talk about it. Let's write about it.

I've had the opportunity to cowrite songs with some of the most talented people on the planet. There is an element of excitement and an element of fear for me in collaborating with someone you admire. Songwriting is very intimate and emotional. You are vulnerable when you are sharing your heart with someone like that. No matter how many songs I've written, I always walk into a songwriting session a little insecure. I guess it keeps me from being too arrogant or too cocky. I always have the sense that the person I'm writing with is better than me. Who knows, maybe they feel the same way. You want to offer your best to each other. When it's a good writing fit, there is nothing in the world like it. It just flows.

The person I love writing with most of all is my friend, Matt Bronleewe. None of that nervousness or angst about whether or not we will be able to write well together exists between us. We get each other. Usually, I'll be sitting on a couch with a laptop open, and he will be sitting at the console facing his monitor working in Pro Tools, the industry standard audio recording and editing program. More often than not, we'll start off our writing sessions with a concept. I might say something like, "I want to write a song about my daughter today," or "I want to write a song about a friend I have who's dealing with the loss of her baby."

Matt may mention an experience that intrigues us both, and we're off running. When a certain idea or feeling connects with me, I can't stop thinking about it until I get it down on paper. It's like therapy for me, and accountability. Matt understands the way I think. He vibes off of what I am thinking about—sometimes on piano, sometimes on guitar—and the song grows out of that. I play piano and guitar like a four-year-old, just well enough to eek out a sound that can inspire me to create an entire song, both lyrics and melody. However, I am awful enough at it that I only play in private, not with another writer. It's a handicap, and if I could make one request of all parents: Please do not let your kids quit piano. You never know how badly they may need it someday. And it will never hurt to know how to play even if they don't do music full time. Who doesn't like to be the person who can play "Happy Birthday" at parties?

Writing songs with Matt is organic, truly good, and so easy. As I begin working on the lyrics, he starts building the song. He usually starts with a beat, either a loop or some kind of rhythm. Then he starts adding a little guitar, then he adds a little bass. He might throw in some bells and whistles before turning and checking in with me.

"How are you doing verse, chorus, and structure-wise?" he'll ask. I'll sing what I have and we'll edit each other. We're not afraid to share what we think with each other. I write best with Matt because I have complete creative freedom with him. Or maybe I write best with him because in all my years in Nashville he's the best neighbor I've ever had.

Tammy, Tara, and I parted ways on the best and most loving terms when our lease was up in April of 1996. Tammy had gotten married in March, and Tara had decided she wanted to move to Franklin. She wanted me to come with her, but I was being frugal. Franklin felt a little too trendy for me so I found a little one bedroom, one bath by myself in Antioch.

It was my first time living completely on my own. I was at a place in my very shiny new career that was pretty frustrating. I was a signed artist with no songs to sing. I had one songwriting credit to my name. It was a song about boogers that my friend Keesha and I had written in junior high. But I was pretty sure "Boogers" wasn't destined to be a hit on my new album.

I had been trying to write with my friend Chris, a guitar player, but it had been more like one song forward, five songs back. It is no easy task to write good songs and way too easy to write crappy ones.

I had been trying to figure out some way to improve my writing process. I felt at a disadvantage not knowing how to play an instrument—as neither my high-school band clarinet skills nor the piano lessons I had taken as a child was going to be enough. I decided I needed to get a guitar. Guitars are portable and great instruments with which to sing along. In high school I had tried playing an extremely junky guitar that had made my fingers bleed. That put me off guitar (bleeding fingers are not my favorite thing). But I had heard from friends that learning to play on a good guitar was easier so I went on a mission to find one. I had $375 saved when I saw the flyer in the apartment mailroom that read "Guitar for Sale." I tore one of the phone numbers off the bottom and went back to my apartment to call Chris.

"Hey, I think I might buy a guitar, and I don't really know what I'm doing," I said. "So, since you play guitar, would you come with me and see if this guitar is worth buying?"

He told me he would be right over.

When Chris showed up, we walked over to the apartment building across the complex. I knocked on the door to a one-bedroom apartment that looked identical to mine. A guy answered the door wearing a Dakota Motor Company T-shirt from an old Christian band I knew. Something to break the ice, I thought.

"Hi, I'm Tiffany. I'm here about the guitar for sale," I said smiling.

"I'm Matt," he said, turning to grab the guitar. His wife was making supper behind him. He let us inside and held out the guitar. "There is nothing wrong with the guitar. We just need to pay our rent."

We laughed. As musicians, both Chris and I understood.

"This is gonna sound really fancy because I just signed a record deal," I said, "but I'm literally no one. No one's heard of me. I need to learn how to write songs, and I figured I'd just buy an acoustic."

Chris looked at the guitar and said, "This is a Takamine. It's a great guitar."

"Would you take $375 for it?" I asked. He would. At this point, it just seemed like too much of a coincidence that he was wearing a Christian T-shirt so I asked, "Are you by any chance a Christian?"

"Yeah, my wife and I both are," he said.

*Small world.* "Well, I am, too."

"So, you say you signed a record deal—with who?"

"Oh, it's no one you've ever heard of," I said. "It's a brand new small label. They only have one artist other than me, really."

"Well, just try me. I'm just curious," Matt said.

"It's called Essential Records."

"Oh, Jars of Clay." He said with a laugh.

I'm not going to lie. I was surprised. "Yeah, you've heard of them?"

"Well, yeah, I used to be in Jars of Clay."

*Even smaller world.* My mouth dropped wide open, "You what?"

"Well, there were four of us in the band. We won a contest, and with that contest, you got a record deal. Before we signed our deal, I was the one out of the four that decided to stay home. I'm the only one that's married, and my heart is really more into producing and writing than it is in performing and touring. So, before I was legally committed to that contract, I left.

"I know all of those Jars guys. I know the label that you're signed to 'cause that's the label I was almost signed to."

All I could say was. "This is crazy." And then I said one more thing. "Well then, will you teach me how to play this guitar?"

"I'd love to."

His wife jumped in next. "You can come over and practice any time."

It seemed too good to be true, but it wasn't. It was real. God does things like that. Completely knocks your socks off with His goodness and His creativity. Only He could have orchestrated Matt and I meeting like that.

My first idea for a song came shortly after that providential meeting. I was still trying to figure out what to write about. I was soaking in the tub, mulling over some thoughts about my high school best friend: Beautiful. Kind. Fun to be around. But her life had been anything but easy. She had never known her biological father, and she had gained a step-dad before she had memory otherwise. He adopted her, but, sadly, he didn't treat her like his own. He constantly compared her to

57

his biological daughter. In his eyes, my friend wasn't beautiful. She wasn't smart. She could never compare. She endured a lot of emotional and verbal abuse during her growing-up years. I had always wanted to fix that for her, to let her know how beautiful and loveable I thought she was.

In a moment, a string of lyrics came to me. I hopped out of the tub to grab a piece of paper and hopped back in so I wouldn't freeze. Hanging over the edge so the paper wouldn't get soaked, I wrote: "I'm never told that I am pretty, I'm never told that I am kind, and my soul burns now with fire inside." The first words, to my first song, "Unforgivable."

The water soaked paper dripped onto the bathroom floor. The essence of the song is in the title. Nothing you have done is unforgivable. No one on this earth is unforgivable. But the sooner you can forgive someone else, the sooner the healing begins in your heart. My pen flew over the paper. The words, the thoughts, were pouring out on it like the bathwater running in streams down the side of the tub. Some songs are written in the studio. Some songs are written in the tub.

When I brought the lyrics to Matt, all that talent bottled up in him came pouring out. He truly is a master producer and songwriter in his own right. When Dan Haseltine, lead singer from Jars of Clay who Essential Records originally hired to make the record, was a no show at the studio one day from an illness, Matt stepped in and began to build the song. They liked what they heard. I loved what I heard. A coincidence? I don't think so. If it sounds unbelievable to you, it felt even more unbelievable to Matt and me. Things like that don't just happen. God knew that Matt and I needed to be next-door neighbors. When the label said Dan wouldn't be back, I petitioned for Matt to have a shot at the job. There was no time to waste. They agreed. And the rest . . . is history. He blew them away.

Our joint effort on "Unforgivable" was the beginning of a beautiful songwriting relationship. Since that song, there has not been an album that I have put together that Matt has not been a part of in some way. His fingerprints are all over my work. And I am thankful for it and him. I always know that good things are going to come when I am songwriting with Matt.

His was one of the friendships I would truly value in the days ahead as I began to tour and build a following. I would rely on it when my music career took an unexpected downturn. One of the things Jeremy says frequently is that life with me is a roller-coaster ride. Never boring. Truer words have never been spoken.

# Chapter 10
## Learning the Business

ONE OF THE BIGGEST parts of being a successful recording artist is having an excellent management team. It's an all-hands-on-deck approach to life and career. Most singers don't think about this when they are starting out. I know I didn't.

"Just get me on a stage and let me do my thing" is the mantra of the newcomer. The problem is that it takes a lot of folks to get you on that stage to do your thing. You don't just go jump on a tour bus. Someone has to rent the bus and hire a driver. You don't just go out on tour. A manager has to book the venues for that tour first.

The tour manager handles everything from getting you on stage at the proper time to overseeing the merchandise table. And it all costs money. You need a gig to pay for it. And you don't just arrive at a gig. A booking agent has to book the gig. You don't just become an overnight sensation. A publicist works behind the scenes booking interviews, sending out press releases, and working with a scheduler to manage your appointments to create that buzz. And as you grow as an artist, your supporting cast grows along with you.

Greatness is a team effort. And all of these different people with their different tasks answer to my manager, Chris, who heads up this grand effort like the ringmaster at Cirque du Plumb. He may manage me as an artist, but he also manages the vision of what Plumb is. He is the one that will politely tell the booking agent, "While Tiffany loves a good polka as much as the next girl, she will be sitting out the Polka Festival," because polka is not where we are headed with Plumb.

He keeps the team focused whether it is helping plan a tour, picking out a new logo for T-shirts, or encouraging me to write my thoughts down in a book. He knows my goal is to share hope with the world through my music and writing every single day of my life. It takes a team of dedicated individuals to spread that hope around. Without them, most of the hope I have to share would remain in my living room or tucked nicely into bed as I take my afternoon nap. I love a good nap.

Plumb isn't a solo act, either. Whether I am on stage singing by myself or with my band, there is an unseen component that is just as vital to the group as I am. My manager calls Plumb a two-person band, with one creative leader and one action-taker. What he's describing is me and my husband, who I affectionately call by his full name, Jeremy Lee. Plumb has the person who lives to perform and connect with the audience, but it also has a person who realizes that if we don't get the bus an oil change and tune-up, we won't make it to the concert to do any performing or connecting. I am the creative part of Plumb and Jeremy is the action-taker of Plumb. He motivates me. I may be the show, but Jeremy Lee gets the show out of bed. He challenges me. He inspires me. And he believes in me even when I don't believe in myself.

When I first started in the music industry, I didn't have Jeremy. I didn't have Chris, my manager. I didn't have a publicist or a scheduler or a booking agent. I had me. I was making decisions that would shape how the next couple of years went, and to say I was naïve as to the workings of the industry would be an understatement. I was young and clueless as to what I needed to do to make a go of a music career. I was figuring everything out as I went along.

My lawyer and my label both told me that I needed a manager. Eventually I listened. After interviewing different managers, I signed on with the same manager and business manager that managed my label mates, Jars of Clay. Looking back, I now realize it would have been better if I had started out with my own management team. It would have provided checks and balances that are good to have in place as an artist. I didn't know that then. At the time it felt good and it was easy. I have always been a fan of easy. Still, the lack of accountability would prove to be trouble later down the road. I had signed with Essential in July, finished writing *and* recording my first record in December, put together a band and a photo shoot and signed with a booking agent and was playing my first shows by April. Whew. That fall I did a double back-to-back tour with Jars of Clay.

I am and will always be a fan of Jars of Clay. Each one of those men is a wonderfully gifted musician; I loved sharing the stage with them. All these years later they are still my dear friends. I grew up with them on the road. I was like a kid sister and they were good big brothers. I remember standing on the stage the first night I opened for them. The air was electric. The seats were packed. The lights overhead were hot and fueled the excitement building inside me. There wasn't a hint of a panic attack on the horizon. The songs I sang were my songs, songs I had worked on for hours with Matt in the studio. These songs had sprung from my pen, and described experiences that had shaped me and made me who I was.

Singing "Unforgivable" on stage for the first time was unreal. There is a feeling you get when you know that the audience is with you on a song. Their faces mirror your own. Your emotion and energy are caught in their eyes. They are sharing in the words, the passion, the delivery of the song.

As I sang the song about my high school BFF it seemed to me that people in the audience were taking it in as their own. They responded with lifted arms and emotion-filled faces, an indescribable moment in time I will never forget. In that first time on stage singing my own songs, I realized I had been made to sing the songs that let people know they are not alone in their pain, but also the songs that let them know there is hope. I was full.

That next year and a half was a whirlwind of activity. My brother moved to Nashville from Texas and became my roommate. I toured twice with Jars of Clay and loved every second of it (seeing my record on the merchandise table for the first time was almost an out-of-body experience). The cover of my record was a simple picture of a plum perched on top of a fork with the word "Plumb" emblazoned across the front. The album was released by both the Christian and general market imprints of my label. It was doing well, too, selling more than one hundred thousand copies. It had been nominated for a couple Dove awards, and the Electronic Dance Music industry had made several dance remixes of my songs. Tracks had also been used in a movie and on television shows.

Life was crazy. Fun. Fantastic. Signing the CDs and meeting with newly won over listeners for the first time was icing on the cake. I was still touring with Jars of Clay and when home, in the studio with Matt. The new muscles I had formed in writing my first album were being used. I was more confident in who I was and who I was becoming.

Recording for the second time was exciting. Each session seemed to build on the last. I was an artist with my faith at my center but with music that seemingly appealed to anyone. And that was fine with me. I was interested in singing to anyone who had ever been lonely or broken-hearted or tossed aside, Christian or not—especially the nots. Hope isn't just for the ones who know their Creator; it's for anyone who feels hopeless. This was my mission: Hope. Hope. And more hope.

I had found my voice, my tribe, my path.

It took only one meeting to upend it all. All the excitement and all the momentum of Plumb came to a screeching halt with the simple announcement, in an otherwise routine afternoon meeting with my manager, that the label would not release my new album unless I used the word "God" on it.

He then handed me a seemingly innocent piece of paper. A fax. Remember faxes? That piece of paper changed the course of my life. We had just completed work on the second album, *candycoatedwaterdrops*, and word had come down from the top that there would be no general market push for this project until it had sold one million copies in the Christian market. The fax was a death knell.

I can remember my heart beating hard. I was angry and confused, and a little nauseated to be honest. "Would they really shelve my album?" I asked. "They know the kind of songs that I write. I love God with all my heart. That is apparent in every song I sing. That doesn't mean I say his name in every song I sing. I don't write like that. That's not me. And this record isn't a typical Christian record, so selling a million copies in that market is literally next to impossible. We've spent more money on this album than anything we've done; I'll never recoup it if they won't promote the album outside the Christian market 'till it sells a million copies,' this is a nightmare." But angry or not there wasn't a whole lot my manager or I could do about the situation.

I was excited about releasing *candycoatedwaterdrops*. I had been welcomed in the Christian market as a Christian, and welcomed by the general market as an artist. Some songs on the new album were about really dark issues, like sexual abuse, that might be difficult to get played on Christian radio, but there were also lighter pop songs about relationships and real life. I wanted to be a part of a revolution in which people loved my music because it was timeless and relevant, not because it was categorized as Christian or not Christian. I wanted to connect with the world, not just with people who believed in Jesus.

On that warm Nashville afternoon, I held a fax in my hand, and I couldn't help but think that if felt like the end. *A million units in a market where they weren't going to play my record since I didn't mention God enough.* No way the record company would recoup the thousands of dollars it had invested in me and the record if the album wasn't released outside of the Christian market. I knew without a shadow of a doubt that this was the end of Plumb. A wave of anger and sadness washed over me. *What could I do?*

In a moment, the dream I'd never dared dreamed had become some terrible nightmare. *How was this possible? How could this have happened?*

The next year would be one of the most difficult of my young life. I reluctantly added a song to the album that mentioned God's name in it, a song I had planned to never play live but rather to just record to soothe the savage beast requiring me to record it. Then, before I knew it, all hell broke loose.

I began to mistrust every member of the team I had built around me. Fear replaced trust. The only time I tried to have a conversation with my team about my concerns it completely backfired on me. My "private" concerns went public, leaked out to the label, and then spread like wildfire throughout the industry.

I felt completely alone. I needed a lawyer. And I needed one fast. My album was finally released, but it wasn't selling near enough to be released by the general market side of my label. My manager and I had a major falling out. Any trust I had placed in him to look out for me had been lost somewhere during all the fallout from that one fax.

Eventually I learned that not only was my record not being supported by the partner that had originally agreed to do just that, but that I was also deeply indebted to both the record company and my manager. Very deep. I, Tiffany Arbuckle, the girl who had saved every penny so I could pay for my car with cash, the girl who had lived debt free (or so she thought), was now tens of thousands of dollars in debt with no viable album to repay it.

On the advice of my lawyer, I filed for Chapter 7 bankruptcy, and found myself at odds with the label I had loved, knee high in depositions and courtroom drama. It seemed like only weeks ago, my life had been painted with a golden hue of success and joy. Now my integrity was being questioned and my life was falling apart. Feeling misunderstood and attacked, I was desperate. *Where was God in all of this?* I was broken, hurting, and feeling run over by life. But I had also found throughout the course of my life that hope often rides in on the heels of our most desperate moments. You just have to hold on.

Little did I know that in that dark place—that place of fear and disappointment and discouragement, of lost dreams and dying wishes—hope was already on its way.

# Chapter 11

## Jeremy Lee

EVEN WHEN I AM at home, I am giving interviews: on television, on the Internet, on the radio. If you haven't figured it out yet, talking is my favorite thing to do. I can talk for days. I don't find interviews tedious. I find it is the one way that I get to share my heart and my story with listeners. Radio stations have been amazing about playing my songs. Their support is vital to an artist. So to spend a few minutes of my day sharing my life and what God has done for me with their listeners is a pleasure.

If you ever have a chance to hear one of these interviews, within the first fifteen minutes of chatting you would probably know three things about me: One, I am beyond grateful for the life God has given me. Two, I like making people laugh by telling awkward stories about myself. And finally, I love Jeremy Lee.

I mean, I love this man with every pore in my body. He makes me laugh. He makes me think. He is a fantastic father to our three kids. He loves Jesus. And he is, hands down, the sexiest man I have ever met. So I am very glad that he is mine.

We are like chocolate and ice cream. On our own we are good. Together we are great. I feel like there is nothing we can't accomplish when we are together. We bring out the best in each other and we balance each other out. I would be very content to spend a great portion of my life napping and wearing sweatpants. Jeremy is going to squeeze the most out of every second of every day that he can. He spends very little time in sweatpants. He has to be on the move, all the time. He often has three projects going at once while I, on the other hand, would be completely happy to spend an entire day just getting a closet organized.

Jeremy lights up when he is around people. He feeds off of their ideas. I need a good chunk of my day to be solitary so that I can refuel and be creative. Jeremy is an explorer, an innovator, and problem solver. I am a relaxer, a romantic, and a creative.

We have had to work hard to bring out the best in each other. Balance isn't something that just happens. You have to practice it. You work at it. You mess up and then you try it again. Jeremy has learned that I really do need to nap to be my best me. And I have learned that Jeremy has to be doing something or he will go stir-crazy. When we were in Amsterdam last year, I came off the plane with jet lag, while Jeremy was completely inspired. There was so much to do and see.

We struck a bargain. He let me sleep for a couple of hours and then he woke me up. We went out and explored the city together. The canals lined with row houses and little shops, the cobbled streets and cyclists. It was amazing.

Being married is like a slumber party and preschool combined. There are always new discoveries being made, new things to take in. Snuggly naps to take. Jeremy Lee and I are still learning each other, and I intend to spend the rest of my life learning Jeremy Lee. I have felt the same way since the first day I met him.

It was December of 1998. I was completely stressed out about my second album, and things were beginning to fall apart with my manager and finances. I needed a break from the craziness of Nashville and from being Plumb. I had been going to a new church my brother had been attending where the college and singles group was planning a ski retreat to Monarch, Colorado. I decided to use the trip as a getaway to focus on my relationship with God. I had been feeling lonely and cynical. It was also the first time I had ever truly felt okay not having a boyfriend. Much of the music business in Nashville is one giant boys' club, and I was a twenty-three-year-old single girl trying to hold her own there. I liked boys. It seemed like I always had a boyfriend or a boy that I liked in tow. But I knew I had used relationships in the past as a security blanket, as a way to feel good about myself. And I didn't want that anymore. So I wrote in my journal a list of every blessing in my life. It read:

1. *I have a cozy apartment that I can afford.*
2. *I have a little Honda Accord that runs great that I paid for myself.*
3. *I have gas in the tank. Money in the bank.*
4. *I have wonderful friends and family.*
5. *I'm healthy.*
6. *I have a great new church that I'm going to.*
7. *I love what I do for a living, in spite of the stress going on right now.*
8. *I've got food in the fridge.*

And I wrote at the end: "You have provided every single thing that I need. Why would you gyp me out of the most important earthly relationship I'll ever have? I don't need a security blanket. You are all I need. And right now, I really need you." I had no idea that God's design that very night was to give me my soul mate, the person who would love me no matter what, who would speak truth into my life no matter what, and who would be the one I could lean on in moments of crisis—not to mention the one who would know precisely what to do when I have a panic attack. I studied the list and took a deep breath. There wasn't a boyfriend on the list, but I kept writing. "I am really thankful. I feel very blessed to have this life You have given me, God. You have overwhelmed me with Your blessings. I trust You."

God has impeccable timing. It was almost like He was waiting for

# Photo Album

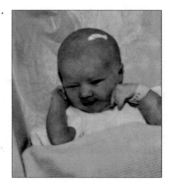

*Newborn Tiffany Lee Arbuckle*

*All smiles*

*First time singing in church with my dad*

*Growing up*

*Senior portrait 1993*

*Cover photo from my first professional
recording in high school, "Called to Belong"*

*Signing my first record deal*

*Recording first Plumb album with
producers Matt Bronleewe and David Haseltime*

*First official Plumb band (left to right): Matt Stanfield, Thad Beaty, me, J.J. Plasencio, and Joe Porter*

*Video shoot in my beloved red velvet pants (before their demise)*

*Monarch, Colorado, ski trip when I (bottom center) met Jeremy (far right)*

JANA CANDLER PHOTOGRAPHY

JANA CANDLER PHOTOGRAPHY

*Dating three weeks*                    *Engagement photo*

*Original wedding, October 14, 2000*

*Ugliest wedding cake ever*

*Original wedding reception*

*Bluefield Avenue, our first married house*

*Oliver, Solomon, and newborn Clementine*

*Solomon Fury, Clementine Fire, and Oliver Canon Lee*

*My "C.C. Bloom," my BFF Melis on her wedding day*

*Unused from the* Need You Now *photo shoot. Originally titled* Faster Than A Bullet *(a line about love from the song "At Arm's Length"), the album name was changed out of respect for the Sandy Hook shootings*

*Changing for our surprise second wedding*

*The kids walk ahead of us for our second wedding*

*The resurrection of a marriage*

*The hope of a new beginning*

*Pre-show makeup 2014*

*Live on tour 2014*

*Plumb 2014 press photo*

*The kids at Pleasant View Montessori 2013*

*On the dock at "the Hope House" with our dog, Buddy*

me to trust Him to be enough so that He could surprise me with His goodness. I love when He does that.

At eight the next morning, a group of us crowded into the youth room at our church as the singles pastor, G. Dale, gave us last minute instructions. I saw my friend, Daveta, bundled in a brown fleecy coat chatting with one of our mutual friends.

"Are you going on the ski trip?" I asked. She was recently engaged, and I had thought she might skip the trip to save for the wedding.

"No, my brother is going," Daveta said.

Now I was more confused. Her brother was thirteen years old.

"Stanton is going on the trip?"

Daveta laughed. "No. My other brother, Jeremy, is going. He's home from college for Christmas break." She pointed out a nearby guy. I read three letters on the back of his T-shirt: "P-l-u." I couldn't see the rest, but it looked like a Plumb shirt. Great. *Just what I need on the trip. A fan.* Her brother turned, still talking to another friend, and I saw his face. His super cute face. And I distinctly recall doing a double take.

My face, on the other hand, had no makeup on. My hair was twisted up in a bun, and I was wearing quite possibly the worst outfit in my closet: tan cord overalls. I had a suitcase packed full of mix-matched ski gear. I had not been looking to impress anyone on this trip. I grabbed my bags and headed for the bus. *I wasn't looking for a super cute guy. Really, God, does he have to be cute? I am trying to focus on you.* Apparently, God had other plans.

On the twenty-three-hour bus ride from Tennessee to Colorado, I couldn't stop looking at my friend's brother: six-foot, broad-shouldered, sandy blond hair, blue eyes, with an infectious laugh. Here I was trying to have a holy weekend away with God, and there's Jeremy pacing the bus like a caged lion, talking to everyone, making it impossible for me not to notice him.

"How does he know everybody?" I asked my friend Tambri.

"Well, he goes to this church . . . he's been gone a few months at college, now home for Christmas break. So even though you haven't met him, everyone else here knows him."

"Well, it's annoying," I said.

She nodded in agreement, "He's kind of hyper."

It was mostly annoying because he was talking to everyone except me. He was laughing and interacting and being way too much fun to be ignored by anyone, least of all me. I found myself keeping tabs on him throughout the night as we headed to the snow.

Halfway into the long bus ride, a group of us started playing Catch Phrase, and Jeremy made his way to the middle of the bus to play with us. Four of us in aisle seats were playing across from each other, and he was seated diagonally to me as my partner. The point of Catch Phrase is to get your partner to guess the phrase on your card by giving clues without actually saying any of the words in the phrase. As Jeremy gave me clues, he kept tapping my knee to get my attention. I have no clue what word he was trying to get me to guess—all I could think was, "I'm never going to guess the answer to this because all I'm thinking about is how much I love you touching my knee."

I can't tell you if we won or lost that game, but I do know when it ended, he ended up asking to sit next to me so we could keep talking. We talked all the way to Colorado.

By the time the bus pulled into the lodge, I had a full-blown crush on Jeremy Lee. I was a year and a half older than him. I lived in a different state than he did. And I had just told God that I didn't need a boyfriend. I was trying desperately to hold my ground and I couldn't. He was too much fun. The next few days we couldn't get enough of being together. We would ski and I would fall, and he would laugh and help me up. He was a snowboarder and I couldn't get past how sexy that was. We hung out and played cards and warmed up with hot chocolate at the lodge. I had three solid days of Jeremy Lee and that was not enough. On our last day together, he pulled me aside and said, "I've got to tell you something."

"Okay."

"Well, it's obvious that there's something between us."

"Yeah." I was trying to be calm as my heart thumped in my chest. It was very obvious. There was really no denying the attraction. And then he said the one thing I never expected . . .

"Well, I have a girlfriend."

"What? Are you serious? You're a jerk!"

Jeremy started laughing at that. Part of me was disappointed because I already liked him so much, but the other part of me was thinking, See, he's young and stupid. You should've stuck with the plan of no guys on the ski trip. Before my thoughts could go any farther down that lane, he interrupted.

"But she is really more of a friend than she is anything else."

"Yeah, right, right."

"No, she really is. I've only been dating her for a couple months. We've only kissed a couple times; it's nothing serious. It's not like she's my wife."

"Oh, and I am?" I chuckled with sarcasm.

"I actually think you might be."

My face went blood red. My heart was beating madly. This was it. This was the guy. I couldn't hear what he had to say next fast enough.

"The reason I haven't held your hand, the reason I didn't kiss you at midnight on New Year's Eve—that's why. I know we've only known each other for a few days," he said, "but it's super obvious that we really like each other. I haven't said anything more than that because I need to break up with her. So let me make that right before we get any more serious."

"Well, you're going to break this girl's heart," I said conflicted. "And how do you know I'd even say, Yes?"

Jeremy grinned, "Because I know you would say, Yes. It's obvious that you would say, Yes."

I couldn't help laughing. I thought, Whoa! Slow it down, buddy. But at the same time, I liked it. I liked the thought of him thinking of me in that way. We had both dated a lot of people over the years, but this boy and I shared a connection I had never felt with anyone else. Like the best friend I've always known but hadn't met, he felt like home.

When we had talked earlier in the trip about what I did for a living I had told him I was a singer. It hadn't seemed to faze him.

"Well, I was born and raised in Nashville; everybody sings, but what do you actually do to pay your bills?"

"I sing."

"Oh, like in the studio or what?"

I was afraid to tell him I was Plumb, because I'd played at his college twice. I thought, if he's a fan or if he's wowed by that at all, that would be a turnoff to me, so I told him.

"Well, it's called Plumb."

"Should I have heard of that?"

I felt a wave of relief roll over me knowing that he had no idea who I was. "Well, I've played at your school twice."

"Really?"

"With Jars of Clay."

"Oh, I remember them playing at our college," he said, "but I didn't go see them."

"Well, I thought your shirt said 'Plumb' when I saw you the first time a few days ago."

"No," he said, with a laugh, "it says, 'Plug.' It's a snowboarding brand."

I laughed with him and said, "I figured that out. And that's way cooler than you having on a Plumb T-shirt."

I felt my world start to tilt a little in that moment. Jeremy Lee liked me. And he wanted me to be his girlfriend. There was not one thing I was not attracted to about him. I liked his honest approach to life. I liked the way his eyes crinkled at the corners when he laughed. I liked his face in general. I liked him. A lot. And the best part was, I saw what I felt for him mirrored in how he looked at me.

He called me after he got back to college and told me about his conversation with his then girlfriend.

"I've told her. I told her that I met someone. . . . about how I'm really interested in you, and broke it off. She took it really well. Was surprisingly understanding. So I'm kind-of officially asking you to continue to pursue this with me."

I thought about it for all of two seconds and said, "Uh . . . yes."

I could hear the smile in his voice when he said, "See, I knew you would."

He knew me already. It was in those early moments of our relationship that we began to learn each other. Study each other. Know each other. God had given me what I had not even thought to request: Someone who would truly love me for me.

What I felt for Jeremy was new and lovely. I couldn't wait to be with him, hold his hand, and kiss his lips. I couldn't wait to talk to him and share my thoughts and my dreams with him. As I said, God has impeccable timing. At the most difficult time in my life, He gave me someone to lean on, to laugh with, and to share my life with. I couldn't wait to get started.

# Chapter 12
## Love Actually

JEREMY AND I ALWAYS plan a date night once a week. It's one of the things that sustains us and nurtures our relationship. Carving out time for dinner by ourselves has become a priority for us. And it's fun. We love trying out new restaurants. A good Indian place or yummy Thai restaurant goes a long way with us. We are restaurant evangelists. Whenever we find a good place to eat—and there are a gazillion good places to eat where we live—we want everyone we know to experience it, too.

Yet while we love date night, finding time to get away can be difficult. With the kids' schedules, our different businesses, studio time, and church life, it seems something is always vying for our time and attention. We have had to learn to prioritize. A night together is like an island of calm in a sea of happy chaos. There is something about eating food together, spending time without the kids, and taking a moment to breathe that feeds our souls, not just our bellies. It knits us together. It reminds us how much we love each other, and why we like being together.

Mother Teresa once said that the hunger for love is much more difficult to remove than the hunger for bread. When I was growing up, I thought love was a simple steady kind of thing that was never in short supply. But life has taught me love can be changeable. Just because I love you doesn't mean that you love me back. It is not a steady or sure thing. Love can be all encompassing or incredibly narrow. It has to be nourished, cared for, and protected for it to grow. To me, real love is about choosing. You choose whom you love and how you love them. Jesus shows us the perfect example of this. He knows us in our mess and still He chooses to love us anyway. Our story starts to get good when we know Him and choose Him back.

There are no cover-ups with real love. Jesus made sure of that. He takes us at our worst and chooses to love us in spite of ourselves. There is a sense of complete honesty and trust and safety that comes from being known completely and being chosen in spite of your faults or flaws. This sense of no cover-ups is what I found so attractive about Jeremy. There were no secrets I wouldn't tell him and none that he wouldn't tell me. We had laid out our pasts in front of each other in a snow lodge in Colorado on those long early morning talks. We kept the truth coming in daily phone calls after he returned to school and I went back to Nashville. He was completely himself with me. I was completely myself with him. I could burp in front of him. I could fart in front of him, which, in my book, meant I felt completely comfortable around him.

He wasn't put off by my earthy nature either. And that was a good thing. I had one of my horrible attacks during his visit home from school. Clutching my stomach, writhing in pain, searching for a bathroom on the way home from a date wasn't super romantic, but Jeremy Lee just took it all in stride. He encouraged me and prayed for me. Several months later, it was Jeremy who first pointed out, "Tif, I think your stomachaches are from anxiety. You said your attacks are happening less and less every year, right?" And they were. And I am pretty sure his presence had something to do with that.

Though we started out long distance dating, we called each other throughout the day to share funny stories or encourage each other or just to hear each other's voice. This wasn't just a crush or a fling. I had dated a lot of people and none of them were like Jeremy. My past relationships were always in some kind of imbalance with one person liking the other person more. There was none of that with Jeremy Lee, but rather a natural easiness about us.

As we began to know each other better, we began to like each other more. Along with the excitement of a new relationship, came the feeling that I had known this person forever. I was settling into something that was good and strong and right. Within weeks of the ski trip, I began to realize that I really, really liked Jeremy Lee. More than I had ever liked anyone else in my life. Even better, I knew he felt the same way about me.

It didn't take long though for our relationship to be put to the test. We had been dating all of six weeks when Jeremy called to say he couldn't come see me that weekend.

"They think I have lung cancer," he said. "They want to admit me for a biopsy. I have to have surgery."

I couldn't believe what I was hearing. When I had driven down to see him a few weeks prior and stayed with his friend Lauren, Jeremy had experienced what he thought was an asthma attack. He was having trouble breathing. It happened again and he had gone to the hospital for tests. Now I was learning the doctors didn't think he had asthma, they thought he had lymphoma sarcoidosis.

I heard the slight tremor of fear in his voice, when he asked, "Can you come?"

"Of course I'll come!" I said, though I had a show that weekend in Bristol, Tennessee, a few hours away.

I was scared. Not because it seemed like Jeremy was asking too much too soon, but because I thought I might lose him before I even had a chance to be with him. Nothing was going to keep me away from being with him. I drove straight from the Bristol show to the hospital.

The sterile smell of hospital filled his room in the pulmonary intensive care unit. His family surrounded his bed. He was hooked up to IVs and monitors. His chest was stitched where they had cut him open. Even in a hospital gown, groggy with pain meds, he was cute. I blinked back the tears and smiled. I didn't want him seeing me scared.

"Hey," he said at the sight of me, flashing his infectious smile.

"Hey," I said taking his hand.

I was seeing Jeremy at his most vulnerable just as he had seen me at mine. It wasn't off-putting or overwhelming. It felt like I was exactly where I should be. He had no worry about me going anywhere.

His parents were kind to me, welcoming me into his room, but I could see the questions in their eyes. His mom later told me why.

"I remember thinking, why is this young girl who's only been dating my son for six weeks all the way here from Nashville at the intensive care unit of this hospital?" And she admitted to me that it had seemed a little premature to her.

My parents had thought the same thing when I told them I was going to be with Jeremy in the ICU. It seemed to them a little early on in the relationship to be committing to something like that. What neither of our parents knew was that in that six-week time frame, both of us had grown to feel so serious about each other that it would have felt weird if I *hadn't* gone to be with Jeremy.

With his incision still healing, Jeremy was going to be in the ICU for a while. His mom, in her great kindness, invited me to stay with her in the room that was provided for family of those in intensive care. The surgeon also shared with Jeremy's parents what needed to happen next.

"We need to go in further to get the cancer out," the doctor told them. "We will open Jeremy from the armpit to the waist, and then break open his ribs to go in and get a better biopsy of it—if not remove all of it. The recovery for this will be pretty extensive."

Cancer has a way of sucking the air out of the room.

Life is crazy, chaotic, and full of surprises, but sometimes those surprises are gifts from heaven. Sometimes the crazy things that happen are the best things that could happen. They are moments of joy and hope that shine through that dark place we know as fear. Before going forward with the invasive surgery, Jeremy's parents decided to send away all his labs and X-rays to a surgeon in Nashville for a second opinion. That decision set us free. The surgeon came back with a different prognosis. The spots on Jeremy's lung X-ray weren't cancer at all. They were spots of histoplasmosis, a fungus found in folks who have grown up around bird droppings or bat guano.

Known also as "Cave disease," histoplasmosis is quite common in middle Tennessee, and so Jeremy's new doctor had seen the infection regularly in his practice. Most people who have grown up in this area have at least a little bit of it in their bodies.

Jeremy was going to be fine. This time the tears that welled up in our eyes were tears of joy. All I could think was, Thank God for bird poop.

With further testing, the doctor was able to confirm the diagnosis down to the retinal scarring from the fungus in Jeremy's eyes. Most people live their entire lives never even realizing that they have histoplasmosis. While the doctors weren't sure Jeremy's breathing problems were related to the fungus, he was free to go home. Life was good. Really good.

Jeremy's parents wanted to bring him home to Nashville to recover from his biopsy. The thought of Jeremy living ten minutes away from me was fantastic. Who would have ever thought I would be glad Jeremy had to have his chest sliced open.

His mom and I played ambulance driver on the way home. We made a pallet in the backseat of my Honda and tucked Jeremy in with a pillow and blanket. Jeremy's mom told me later, "I had no idea that I was sitting in the car with my daughter-in-law. I just thought this was a really nice girl who's dating my son, but my son dates a lot of girls." I, on the other hand, was thinking, "If this ends up being my husband, this will be a story that we will never forget."

And we haven't forgotten it. Sometimes pain or fear or an obstacle faced together can separate you from the one you love. Other times it knits your hearts closer, tightening the bonds that have already begun to form. Before Jeremy got sick, I knew I liked him. After he got sick, I knew I was falling in love with him. It was a defining moment for us. His moving back to Nashville only served to cement our relationship.

My career might have been unraveling and uncertain times might lay ahead, but I was grounded in the fact that I had found the one person I wanted to be with for the rest of my life. We hadn't told each other we loved each other yet, but I was choosing Jeremy Lee. And that was a beautiful thing.

# Chapter 13
## My Own Version of *Beaches*

W HEN I RETURN home from a long tour, the normal routine of life feels like it's disappeared. I have to figure out how to work my way back into everyday living. My sleeping hours flip-flop. Instead of late nights and late mornings with concerts, it's early evenings and early mornings with kids. Instead of signing autographs and eating via a catering service, it's helping with homework and making supper. Instead of singing on stage, it's writing and recording in the studio.

One thing seems to get my head back in the right place when I am home, and that is spending time with my best friend, Melis. I've been known to take her on tour with me, which is beyond fun, but I find there is nothing like being home with her, putting on our sweats, curling up on the couch with a chick flick, and laughing 'til our ribs hurt or crying our eyes out together. We get each other. That is a rare and fantastic thing to have in this world.

Melis is hands down one of the top five people in the world who has made me who I am. She's made me more moldable, shapable, changeable. How do I love Melis? Let me count the ways. She's made me more likely to admit my faults and change them. She is big on taking ownership of your own stuff. She loves me tough. She's not a Yes person who is going to just compliment me or brag on me. She tells me what she honestly thinks about me, about the world, and about God. Melis is wise, she listens, she is flexible, and more often than not, unselfish. Whether I'm throwing a birthday party or feeling sick, whether I need a babysitter or some advice, she's willing to do whatever it takes within the confines of what she's able to do. There is nothing gross or weird that I have done that she doesn't know about and she loves me anyway. And of course, there is the fact that she makes me laugh harder than anyone in the world. There is that.

Once when we stopped to use a public restroom, I was already in the stall when she came in. Every time Melis walks into a public restroom, she makes a "pffft" sound, a sort of greeting fart, to let you know she is in the room with you. So I heard "pffft" and then I heard the stall door next to me close. A minute later I heard a genuine bodily function sound that echoed off the concrete walls surrounding us—no pffft required. I started laughing.

"Melis, is that you?"

There was an ominous three-second silence.

"Uhhhh, no."

I almost died. Apparently, someone else was letting it rip close by. I almost had a seizure trying not to laugh. I could not get out of there fast enough. When Melis joined me outside, we were both wiping tears from our eyes. The funny part wasn't the random farting we had just overheard, but the classic response, "Uhhhh, no." It has morphed its way into our everyday "yes" and "no" vernacular. Even Clementine uses it.

"Clementine, did you clean your room?"

"Uhhhh, no."

"Are you going to?"

"Uhhhh, yes."

It's just one of the many reasons I love Melis. What's funny is that when Jeremy and I first met Melis, she clicked more with him. She

81

gravitated to him like a kid sister. They had a mutual friend, Jeremy's best friend, (Jason) Dodge, from college. When Melis was living out her hippy years, playing and singing in a band, she and two friends loaded up their car and moved to Nashville the summer between their junior and senior year—just because it seemed fun. And it was.

It was Dodge who had told Melis to look us up when she got to Nashville. He slipped her Jeremy's number on a piece of paper, and she shoved it in her pocket. She knew Jeremy was dating me and she'd heard of me through a DJ at her college radio station. Crashing at the house of some friends' parents, she decided to give Jeremy a call.

This was only a few months after Jeremy's cancer scare, and we had completely fallen for each other by this point. Jeremy was learning about the industry and starting to work at a business management firm managing the money of musicians. I was knee-deep in bankruptcy and dinner at a TGI Fridays with a new friend was a bright spot, something to be enjoyed. We talked music and industry news. Melis and her friends were in a band together. They didn't know that much about the business side of music yet; they just wanted to play. It was fun hanging out, laughing, sharing ideas.

"Why don't you guys come to church with us this Sunday?" I asked before leaving.

They accepted, and that Sunday at church cemented our friendship. We were inseparable the whole summer. We found studio space for Melis's band, and I tried my hand at producing, giving them suggestions and sharing any wisdom I had come by over the last few years. We ate together. Went to church together. Saw movies together. Shared life together. Melis told me later that she thought I was killing it at the time, that I had my act together. I didn't have a manager anymore so I was independent and managing my career. She was still an irresponsible college student couch surfing at a friend's house. She thought that I was brave. She was drawn to that about me, and I was drawn to her sense of humor and intellect. Melis knew more about music groups and theology than I had ever taken time to think about. When she and Jeremy were deep in discussion about culture, I was soaking it all in. This was a girl I loved being around. She wasn't prissy. She was real and authentic and smart. With both Melis and I, what you see is what you get. I connected with that in her.

At that point in time, we had no clue that our lives would be woven together so intricately. Melis was returning to school in the fall. But the connection we formed that summer has spanned the fifteen years since. Jeremy and I went to her college graduation. I was thrilled when she moved to Nashville. Life got better when Melis showed up. We have watched each other fall in love and get married. Melis has been at the births of all of my children and loves them like they are her own. She is their "Meme" and they don't know a life without her.

Melis and I know each other's deepest secrets, saddest sorrows, and greatest joys. We have weathered countless crises together and leaned on each other when things grew difficult. We are like sisters except better because we have chosen each other. God knew that I needed Melis in my life. He knew that she needed me in hers. One of the ways that He loves us best is by placing people in our lives who challenge us, who keep us accountable, who laugh with us, and who love us no matter what.

One of our favorite movies ever is *Beaches*, the story of two women, C.C. Bloom and Hillary, who meet at the boardwalk one summer and form a friendship that endures from childhood through adulthood. The two women could not be more different in temperament or outlook, but their relationship is honest and hard and beautiful. Their love for each other is the glue that gets them through life. When Hillary is dying of cancer, C.C. is the one she turns to, asking her friend to raise her daughter and to carry on her legacy. Like C.C. Bloom and Hillary, Melis and I are complete opposites in a lot of ways, but our personalities, our strengths, our gifts complement each other.

The similarities in how we enjoy life make hanging out the best thing in the world. We both love to have a hot cup of coffee or tea. We both love to watch all kinds of movies. We both love to get massages and pedicures. We both love to stay up late talking. We both love the beach. And we both love each other. The more years that we have together, the more experiences and the more memories we share, and that further solidifies our friendship. It just gets better. Even when it's hard, it gets better. Next to Jeremy Lee, Melis is the person who knows me best. And when I've needed her most of all, she has always been right there. She's my rock. She's my C.C. Bloom even though I'm the one who sings for a living and has the crazy curly hair.

# Chapter 14
## Wedding Bells

AS FAR AS I AM CONCERNED, Jeremy Lee is brilliant. I may be a little biased in my opinion because he is so hot, but there's really nothing that the man cannot do. He's an incredibly hard worker, natural learner, and leader. If he doesn't know how to do something, he will research it until he figures out how to do it. In the course of our marriage, he has worked as a business manager, a warehouse manager, a house remodeler, a floor refinisher, a music publisher, a music manager, an overseas importer, a school developer, and the list goes on. I am one hundred percent convinced that if Jeremy really wants to do something, he will figure out a way to get it done and get it done right, and it will be creative and quality and thoughtful and pure Jeremy Lee. I know this because I have seen him to do it over and over again. And even though he may not claim to be a hopeless romantic, he has pulled off some of the most romantic surprises I have ever had, like the time he threw me the best birthday party of my life.

We had been dating for more than a year when I rounded the corner on my twenty-fifth birthday. Jeremy had invited my closest friends, my parents, and his mom to Tara's house (you know, my former room-mate and later maid of honor), and instead of a gift, he had asked them to bring a candle in one of my favorite colors, along with a special memory of me to share. He had two different people make cakes and orchestrated everything without one hint from me. I actually had no clue what was coming.

So there I sat encircled by my dearest friends and family caught up in this amazing moment of love, as each of them stood and lit their candle and shared a special thought or memory about me. Tara went first, and I was crying before she lit the candle; I was still weepy at the end when Jeremy closed it all out by sharing the birthday card he had written to me.

"Tiffany, we have been through a lot together in this past year," he began, and all I could think was, Oh my word, he is going to propose to me right now! This is the best night of my life!

. . . Until he finished reading his card, and I realized he was not go-ing to propose to me, at least not that night. That was a different kind of surprise. Up to that point, it was still the best night of my life. I had found the person with whom I fit. I knew Jeremy was the one that I wanted to spend the rest of my life with . . .

My parents, on the other hand, weren't so certain. These two people who I love so dearly had never had to *really* let go of their only baby girl. And as much as they liked Jeremy, they pulled out the apron strings, altered to a shorter, tighter length. My relationship with my parents became strained. I would spend the better half of my life trying to find a new healthy balance between being wife first and mother second and still a daughter. It has been one of the more difficult things I've ever had to experience, which came as a bit of a shock given the hopelessly romantic vision I had for finding the one I would marry. I imagine my parents would tell you they feel differently now than they did then.

That summer Jeremy and I did a lot of picnicking at our favorite spot in Centennial Park. That shady patch of grass under a canopy of trees is where he first told me he loved me on June 2, 1999. We had made it our regular place to have lunch on his day off. It was a good place to talk and kiss and kiss and talk. We talked a lot about getting married. How much we loved each other. How much fun it would be to climb into the same bed at night and wake up in the morning together. We talked about Plumb and what that would be like once we were married. Jeremy was already looking into figuring out how to start a publishing company so we could publish our own songs. Like I said, he is brilliant.

At the moment, I was unsigned and just playing a few dates here and there. The bankruptcy ordeal was over, however, and I was broke. Or maybe I should say I was broke and rich at the same time. I was rich because of what Jeremy and I had together. We had each other. We had hope and an amazing future ahead of us.

One early Tuesday morning (remember 8 a.m. is early for me) I was awakened by a knock at the door. It was Jeremy Lee. He handed me a card, gave me a quick kiss, and took off. With eyes still not quite in focus I read the card. It was sweet. That afternoon, he picked me up to grab lunch at one of our favorite lunch places, Ham 'n Goodys. (They have amazing tea cake cookies.) After we got our food to go Jeremy asked, "I know that you don't want to go ring shopping because you want to be surprised but can we just look one time at the jewelry store across the street? It'll be sorta fun. Just to give me some ideas?"

I agreed even though what he said was true: I did want to be surprised and swept off my feet. I loved the thought of him picking out my ring. Still, we went in to check out the rings. I pointed out a few that I liked.

"I like this one. This is pretty. And this one is nice. Anyway, let's go! I'm hungry."

And we headed to our spot in the park.

As we were walking, we held hands, and I noticed Jeremy's seemed clammy.

"Do you feel okay?"

"Yeah, why?"

"Your hand feels clammy. Are you getting sick?"

"No, I'm not sick."

The sun was warming the grass as we got to our spot and sat down. I spread out our lunch and popped the top on a root beer, root beer being my favorite drink of all time. The air was warm and a little humid. It was June—June 20, 2000, to be exact. We'd been chatting for a little bit when Jeremy asked, "Do you trust me?"

"Yeah," I said.

Tapping my knee, he asked, "Do you really trust me, like with your life?"

"Yes," I said.

He grinned. "Well I know that we've been dating for a year and a half. We've been talking about marriage for a little while, and I just don't want you to feel like, 'Is he ever going to ask me? Is he really in this?' "

"I know you are," I said.

As I mentioned, my parents had had a change of heart when it came to letting go of me. It had little to do with Jeremy and more to do with them. Although I had wanted the fairy tale, my dad had not given us his blessing. Something I'm sure he now regrets.

I watched Jeremy start to get up on his knees as if he were going to adjust his belt, but instead he stayed on one knee and pulled a gray velvet box out of his pocket. He caught me completely off guard. "Tiffany, I love you. Will you please be my wife? Will you marry me?"

"Yes, yes, yes!"

That was all I could get out—about nineteen times I repeated it. Now my hands were clammy. Jeremy Lee put the ring on my finger. We both drew up and onto our knees and hugged and kissed. And cried. And kissed. And prayed together. And kissed.

We prayed that day that God would bless this marriage and this new season and each other. And then we cried and kissed some more.

"I want you to look over there," Jeremy said.

I turned and I looked, but all I saw was an old parked Volvo.

"What? That Volvo?"

"No, not the Volvo. Look right past it," he said. And there they were: Tara and Tammy, hiding in the bushes. One was filming the

88

whole thing, and the other one was taking pictures. Our moment had just been made even more special. At that point, Tara and Tammy came running over, and we hugged and cried some more. This had just become the new best day of my life.

I was going to be Mrs. Jeremy Lee.

We were engaged that day and married three and a half months later on October 14. We honeymooned in Venice, Italy, and New York City. Only two things fell short of perfection: One was our wedding cake. It was supposed to be a Renaissance castle with a real moat but ended up looking like a disco cake from the Eighties. Where the moat should have been it had clear plastic pillars with lava lamp bubbles shooting out. And then there was the wedding night.

Being a virgin, I had high expectations for the night. *Really high.* What I wasn't prepared for was how incredibly painful it would be, more like a medical procedure than a romantic act of passion, if you asked me. I found myself being so thankful I was with Jeremy Lee for it. It wasn't embarrassing. It wasn't awkward. Ironically, it was incredibly bonding. We even laughed at one point, like, Are we doing this right?

It is something I am grateful no one else but Jeremy will ever experience with me. In the moments of temptation before him, even the times that I'd maybe gone too far, I had certainly not gone this far. And I was safe, with the first and only person to know me this well. Jeremy was more than understanding about everything—"Tif, it's okay," he said, as he held me. "We have a lifetime to get this right." I meanwhile was a little bummed. *We had waited all these years for this?*

It took three and a half more years before we discovered that all my pain that night was caused from the birth-control medication I was on. With the blessing of my chiropractor, I stopped taking it. When I had sex for the first time without pain, I wept tears of relief and joy, knowing that, This is what it is supposed to be like! Our struggle through those first years only drew Jeremy and me closer. We were completely in love. However, after we figured it out, we made sure to make up for lost time.

When we returned home from our honeymoon, we began what we like to call the perpetual slumber party. We moved into a darling little rental on Fairfield Avenue. It sat on a corner lot with a backyard and a carport. Before we knew it we were parents to a couple of adorable Weimaraners, Monarch and Venice (as in Colorado and Italy). The dogs just added to the joy.

We were the first of our group of friends to get married, so our house became the house where everyone would come over and hang out, especially on the weekends. We had barbecues and game nights. We were spontaneous, always traveling, trying out new restaurants, and going to movies. It seemed almost like a grown-up version of college life in the best possible way. We were very involved in church and with the youth group. We were thrilled to be married. And we were content.

Our friends would tell us, "Man, I hope we have what you guys have one day. It just seems like it's fun all the time." And it was. Life was good. Every hope I had of what marriage could be was happening. I was spending my days with my best friend. I loved my life.

Right before our wedding Jeremy had started work as a warehouse manager, and he had to be at work by 6:00 a.m. So, being the Donna Reed-wanna-be that I am I got up every morning at 4:48 a.m. to make him fried bologna and eggs, his favorite. I'm a night owl, so I was being "sacrificial." That lasted all of two weeks. Soon I began staying up later and sleeping in until 11:00 a.m. I told myself I had put in my time, and I would be a better wife to Jeremy if I got my much-needed rest. He may or may not have agreed with that.

After the first year we bought our first home on Bluefield Avenue. We brought our cute little Weimaraners with us. We knew by now that we liked being together. Not just in the good, but in the bad and the ugly and even the gross.

One of our earliest bonding moments came in a shared case of food poisoning. We were miles away from our one-bathroom home when I announced, "I think I am going to have diarrhea."

"I think I am going to have diarrhea, too!" Jeremy said.

"Jeremy! You know I am the one with stomach issues."

"No, I really think I am going to be sick," he said.

We ended up sick at the same time and taking turnsies on the toilet, as the other waited their turn perched on the rim of the bathtub. This may not be something you would normally think would be funny. Except that we couldn't stop laughing. The sights and sounds and smells of the event will live in a happy place in our minds forever. Even being sick was better being married.

Jeremy started renovating Bluefield, redoing the floors and the kitchen. We were making this house a home. And he was good at it. He realized that he could do a couple of renovating jobs a month and make the same amount he was making in the warehouse in a week. So we said bye-bye to the warehouse.

He also continued to teach himself the music publishing business. Having worked at a business management firm when we dated, Jeremy had learned a lot about the music business as he dealt with the finances of artists. Meanwhile I began writing for other artists, not just myself. For the first time, I also owned the rights to my own music. Jeremy managed all of the details of the business, and I did the creative work. I wrote the songs; he pitched them to artists and got them recorded. He hung the dry wall and I held the nails.

We were a true team.

One of my first songs that I owned the publishing rights to was a song I wrote for Mandy Moore. When the first check came in made out to my maiden name, I surprised Jeremy and took him to a motorcycle shop for a test drive.

"Will you be driving this home or do you need someone to drive it home for you?" asked the salesman.

"Oh, no! I was just trying it out," Jeremy said.

"Um, no, your wife bought this for you. Would you like to drive it home?"

I pocketed a lot of good wife points for that surprise, even if I no longer got up early to make him fried bologna and eggs over medium.

I remember us hearing someone bemoan one time how hard the first year of marriage is. All we could say was, "What? It's amazing! It is the party that never stops." Everything about married lifee was exciting and new for us.

By the end of our first year of marriage, it had become clear that Jeremy had a lot more to offer this world than he thought. He was finding his passion didn't revolve around sanding floors. His dreams were lining up with my own. Even though I was disappointed about how things had gone down with my last record deal, Jeremy was finding his niche in the music industry. It wasn't long before he began focusing on our new company Weimarhymes Publishing and managing what was left of my career. These first years were sweet and golden, like honey. We were young, full of hope, and full of love. We couldn't wait to see what came next.

# Chapter 15
## Plumb's Girls

ONE OF MY FAVORITE things to do is to go to the movies. Whether it's a chick flick or a suspenseful drama or a laugh-out-loud comedy or an indie film or a documentary, it's a total escape for me. In the dark, with surround sound, drawn in by the giant screen, popcorn in my lap, I am caught up in the stories of other people's lives. I love everything about movies. I love the costumes, the storylines, even the soundtracks. Movies are magical, plunging you into another world, inviting you to feel and hope for the characters.

Jeremy Lee loves movies as much as I do. We have passed this passion on to our children. I see the wonder on their faces when they are watching a story come to life. They have gone through a *Lord of the Rings* phase recently. You've been there. You are hoping beyond hope that Frodo completes his journey of saving Middle Earth despite all the evil surrounding him. You can't help being sucked into his adventures, his triumphs, and his struggles. If you're like me, you find something terrifying and wonderful about the battle of light and dark, good and evil, beauty and ugliness that plays out in these movies.

I find these same themes of light and dark and despair and beauty wind themselves repeatedly throughout the story of my life and the stories of the people that I love. And, of course, they have found their way into my songs. The movie soundtrack of my life would have peaks and valleys, angst riddled melodies, and anthems of hope, all intertwined. It is how life seems to be woven together.

Some people only like to watch movies that are light hearted or frivolous, but some of my favorite movies of all time are Tim Burton's movies. I love his aesthetic: the darkness, the weirdness, and the larger than life characters. There's something so beautiful in the mix of those elements coming together. There's dark. There's light. There's pain so palpable it makes you wince. There's comic relief. It's an oxymoron. You have this dark, messed up character in *Edward Scissorhands*, an abandoned child turned deformed recluse who makes the most beautiful creations with his dangerous weapon-like hands. He keeps hurting himself and he is afraid to hurt other people. He is so clearly wounded and troubled but you find yourself rooting for him to find love. You want him to emerge from his creepy cobwebby attic and find out that he is lovable. You want him to be embraced. You want him to find peace.

Maybe I love the magic of *Edward Scissorhands* so much because he represents all of us. We all have something that makes us unique. We all have something that makes us a little broken and a little weird. But we all want that moment when we are found and someone says, Hey, you live up on the hill in a castle with crazy black hair and scissors for hands, but you know what, come join the party. Be a part of our family and find out what love is because amidst all this darkness and pain and suffering, there is always hope to be found.

From a poetic standpoint, it's the darkness that most often inspires my songs. I would never want to exploit someone's pain but I have always thought that music was an incredible tool to create conversation and, in turn, help people open up about their pain. And through those conversations, healing and hope can be born. I have a certain connection with my listeners because of the types of songs I write. Whether it's a song about cutting or sexual abuse or alcoholism, I have found that singing about these topics shoots an arrow of light into a dark place for them. In a place where they have been hurt so deeply, these songs invite them to talk about their hurt and not be afraid of being rejected or ignored. For some of them, it is a life-giving experience to hear these songs, like taking a long cool drink of water after being parched and dry. I can recognize these listeners when I am at the merch table (where all the merchandise is sold) after a concert. I see them in line before they get to me. I recognize the look in their eyes, their demeanor, their posture. I see the tears on their cheeks and I cry with them. They are "damaged." They are not only girls but, more often than not, they are, and I affectionately call them "my girls."

These are the girls that come to me and say, "I was sexually abused. I didn't think I was going to make it but then I heard your song. It was a turning point for me." Or they find me and say, "I didn't think anyone understood what I was going through until I heard you sing those words. I have been battling an addiction. You helped me realize I am not alone. Thank you for writing that song." Or, "You will never know what this song means to me. It saved my life."

This isn't about being a fan. It's about being connected. By pain. By suffering. And by hope. I never take these moments for granted. And I never take ownership of them. I tell them, "I'm glad that you felt that way, and you need to know that the connection you're feeling is Jesus—it's Him, letting you know you are not alone. He is the one who is speaking to your heart." I tell them this because these are the moments when God is at work. I may have been the instrument singing the song, but it is His spirit at work in these girls' hearts. It is His hope and truth that fills them. I may have held the pen but the lyrics are inspired by Him. He is the one who is saving their lives.

My love for "my girls" is not a one-way street. Plumb's girls keep me accountable. They keep me writing in a place that is honest and true and sacred. They motivate me. And even when they think it's my words encouraging them, it's really their words that encourage me.

I will never forget one particular event when one of these girls shot an arrow of hope into my dark night. I have never been the same since.

It happened while I was still finishing some stand-alone concert dates after the fallout with my first record company. Chapter 7 bankruptcy had been settled but I still had a few shows to play. I was no longer signed to a label but honoring the concerts that had already been scheduled.

Disillusioned with the politics and business aspect of the music industry, I found the whole experience had left a bitter taste in my mouth. I felt my integrity had been called into question and I could hardly stand it. I was angry and bitter. Even though I had been receiving various offers from other labels, I was ready to quit and get out of the industry for good. I just didn't want to do it anymore. My listeners didn't know it, but I thought I was about to do my last concert as Plumb. The marketing of Jesus made me sick. And I felt like somehow I had succumbed to participating in it. I wanted out.

I showed up at a bookstore to sign CDs before that night's concert. It was May of 2001. A runner, a person who helps shuttle people to and from the event, had given my team and me a ride there. Disenchanted with the industry, I was still thankful for the people who loved listening to Plumb and who would be there that night. That is one thing that I never took for granted. But in my heart, it felt like everything else was coming to an end: Tonight's show might well be my last show. This could be my last time to sign autographs. As that thought flitted through my mind, I lifted my head from signing a CD to see one of my girls coming through the line. One of Plumb's girls. Her demeanor and the look in her eyes told me all that I needed to know. She was very different than everyone else asking for an autograph or giving me a quick two-sentence compliment. As I signed her CD, she slid an envelope across the table to me. Her voice caught as she said, "Your music has changed my life. I just want you to read this letter when you get a chance; I won't take up any more of your time." I took the envelope and thanked her and kept the line moving since I only had a few minutes until I had to leave for the venue. As I made my way to the runner's car, I slipped the envelope out of my pocket and broke the seal with my finger.

Sliding into the backseat of the car, I read her first words. Something broke inside of me. I am not a huge crier, especially sitting with a strange person in the car, but as I read her letter, I was undone. Tears streamed down my cheeks, and I read the letter through the blur of tears.

*Dear Plumb,*
*Your song "Damaged" has changed my life. I have been*
*sexually abused so I completely relate to it. Even though it*
*has been so hard, your song has impacted me in a positive*
*way. I don't feel alone anymore. And I have started feeling*
*hopeful again.*

*I have been connecting with other people who have been*
*abused and I have been encouraging them, too. I have even*
*been in a play where I play a girl that has been abused. I*
*have asked the director if we can play the song "Damaged"*
*at the end of the play.*

*You will never know how much your song has changed me*
*and how much it has meant to me.*

All the pain, the embarrassment, and the hurt of the past two years started to shift as I read those words. All that I had ever hoped for as a songwriter was to connect on a deeper level with some of my listeners. When I was first starting out, my publicist had asked me, "Who is your audience? Who are you trying to reach? What demographic are you singing to?" I didn't know at the time. I was just figuring it out as I went along. But all of those questions my publicist asked me were answered in this moment.

This girl had felt what I'd written. This song had done for her what I had always hoped my songs would do. It had connected with her in a way that helped her feel less alone, knowing that someone else related to what she had gone through. And, in turn, she was letting God make beauty from the ashes of her life: not letting her past dictate her future, not letting the bad things that had happened to her cause her to wither away and become bitter and sad and angry but instead letting them make her stronger and smarter and braver and bolder. She had done just that, and at the close of the letter she wrote:

> *I don't know where you are at in your career, but I just know*
> *that what you've done God has really used to change my life*
> *and I really hope you don't stop.*
> *Love, Breanna*

Just as the words of my song had pierced her heart, the words of her letter pierced mine. I sat in the back of the big black Suburban, humbled. Our situations were worlds apart. But she was calling me out. Here I was ready to quit because I had been hurt. But she hadn't quit when she was hurt. She hadn't let the bruises and pain of her life stop her from becoming all God had meant her to become. How could I let the ugliness that had happened in my life keep me from becoming all God had meant for me to be?

The bitterness, the anger, especially the bad attitude faded into a new place of peace. Her words were healing my heart, reminding me one more time that the things that the enemy would like to use for bad, God can always use for the good of those who love him.

That night as I sang my set, I couldn't stop thinking about Breanna and her letter. Under the heat of lights, before I played "Damaged" for what might be the last time, I shared the story of receiving her letter that day and I asked from the stage: "Breanna, if you're in the audience tonight, could you please come backstage and meet me? I loved your letter and I want to talk to you."

After the show, Breanna found her way backstage, and someone led her to my dressing room. I shared with her what I had been going through. "I don't know if this means I will ever sign another record deal. I don't know if this means I will ever play another concert, but I just know that God has used you to change my attitude, and to, more or less, check me. And so, as much as I've tried to inspire and encourage fans, you have come back and inspired me just as much times ten."

Three weeks later, after that backstage meeting, I read another letter that changed my life. It was an offer from my current label, Curb Records. The few other offers I had received I had turned down immediately—I could tell from their cover letters alone they were not the next best step for me. However, as I opened the offer from Curb Records, it was different. It was an offer that spoke very clearly to my heart. I had peace. This is worth signing; this is something I should do, I thought.

One thing for sure—whether or not I was finished being Plumb— God wasn't finished with me being Plumb. He still had things He wanted me to say, words He wanted me to write, and songs He wanted me to sing. I was in it for the long haul.

# Chapter 16
## Giving Birth

MAKING A NEW RECORD is a huge undertaking. It is both terrifying and exciting and all-encompassing and exhausting. There are a million different details to take into account—from the stories I feel compelled to share with the crowd to how we want it to sound sonically from booking the studio to finding the right art for the album cover.

So many people have their hands on the album: From Matt, who most often is producing it, to my cowriters, who I invite to write with me for it, to Jeremy, who inspires so much of its direction, to both my manger Chris and my A&R guy, Bryan, who help to build the team we place around it to make it all happen as seamlessly as possible. And this doesn't actually take into account all of the energy and creativity that goes into launching an album with marketing, publicity, and touring.

It's very much like pregnancy and giving birth. There is a long gestational period. There's a lot of pain and anguish involved before it actually comes to pass. There's a lot of love and expectation wrapped up in the project. And in the end, after all you've invested in the record with your time and money, your creative abilities and a great deal of your heart, you are really just hoping that this album looks a little bit like you—that it captures the essence of who you are and connects with the people you love.

Looking back over the last sixteen years of making records, I have certain sentiments and affections attached to each album. Each album has been a work born out of my view of life, my passion for sharing real stories put to music with my listeners, and the great belief I have that even when the world feels dark, there is hope to be found. I have birthed six albums: *Plumb* (1997), *candycoatedwaterdrops* (1999), *Beautiful Lumps of Coal* (2003), *Chaotic Resolve* (2006), *Blink* (2007), and *Need You Now* (2013). Each one reflects a different time frame of my life and a different part of who I am.

*Plumb* recalls that incredible season of just starting out, not quite knowing who I was as an artist yet but being incredibly excited to find out. It was all about newness and discovery, while *candycoatedwaterdrops* reminds me of feeling more confident in who I wanted to become artistically and how I lost my footing so fast with the Chapter 7 bankruptcy and subsequent loss. *Beautiful Lumps of Coal* reminds me of how mistakes are simply teachable moments if you allow them to be—a new beginning, a second chance.

*Chaotic Resolve* reminds me of how God makes beauty from our mess and gives us direction when we've strayed off course. It reminds me of grace and forgiveness and community. *Blink* reminds me daily of one of the biggest gifts in my life, that of being a mother. It reminds me to not let this sweet time pass me by and to savor every moment, no matter the season.

And *Need You Now?* Wow, it reminds me of more than I ever thought it would. It defined me as an artist. Not that the others didn't have their moments of chipping away to get to the core of who I am. But by *Need You Now*, I was finally Plumb.

Each record is special to me. I love that I can chart the seasons of my life by the records I was working on at the time. For instance *Blink*, my lullaby album, reminds me of the season of my babies. That was a different kind of season all together. From the moment we embarked on the journey of parenthood, we have been in for the ride of our lives.

In the fall of 2004, Jeremy and I were expecting our first child. We were ecstatic. We were in a good season of life. *Beautiful Lumps of Coal* had come out. We had just bought and renovated our first home. He had truly become my partner in Plumb, managing me and running all the behind the scene aspects of my tours, my record-making process, and my publishing. In many ways he was the driving the force behind all Plumb was becoming.

Jeremy has always been a visionary. It's how he's wired. He has a million ideas about how to make things run and how to improve on what we are already doing, and he likes to have different projects going at once. It feeds his soul. Plumb isn't his only outlet. I laugh at how opposite he and I are in so many ways.

My focus had narrowed to one thing: The small person growing inside my belly. The baby was my sole project. The roll and fall of my stomach as I lay on my bed at night mesmerized me. I was memorizing this little one before I had even met him. I was in love with this little person that Jeremy and I had created. I couldn't wait to meet him or her. We waited until delivery on all three of our children to find out if they were a boy or a girl. The surprise is unparalleled to any surprise we've ever experienced.

I may have mentioned a time or twelve that I am a romantic. I had a definite idea of what the birth would be like. I wanted a natural birth. A simple, beautiful, natural, non-drug induced experience that we could look back and marvel at as we cradled our firstborn. I planned to use an exercise ball or shower or walk to refocus my attention when I had contractions.

Our midwife would be there to guide us in a non-medicinal, lovely way as I let my body do what women's bodies have done for centuries without shots, Pitocin, or forceps. I would breathe and hold Jeremy's hand and look into his eyes as we welcomed our newborn into the world. This is what I envisioned for myself. I was soon to learn that babies have minds of their own. They don't really care what we envision.

My water broke on Sunday afternoon, drizzling down my leg into my fuzzy cheetah slippers. Jeremy and I were in the driveway talking to one of my favorite co-writing partners, Christa Wells. I thought at first I might have peed myself. I wasn't uncomfortable but I was aware. So aware that I don't think I even said bye to Christa.

If memory serves me right, I just kind of walked inside the house hoping Jeremy Lee would cover for me and bid her farewell as I ran to get the video camera. I took a bath. I took a nap. We went out to dinner. We went and bought a rug. Stopped by T.J. Maxx and grabbed a new red suitcase. My contractions felt like mild Braxton Hicks pre-labor pains. I told Jeremy, as we timed them, "I'm not in pain. And they're still fifteen minutes apart."

When I went to bed that night, I was pretty excited. I knew that we would be meeting our baby soon. Monday morning, I called the midwife and told her, "Hey, my water broke yesterday afternoon. At least a little bit of it did. I'm not miserable but I'm just super tired. I have an appointment to be there at 9:30 this morning. Could I postpone it and sleep until I get uncomfortable?"

They agreed and set an appointment for 1:00 pm. After the examination, feeling certain I was probably at a six or seven, I was shocked to hear otherwise from the midwife.

"You're maybe at a one. Sadly, we are going to need to admit you."

"Wait a minute. I'm not even in horrible pain."

She placed a hand on my arm. She was understanding, yet firm, "Because your water has actually broken for an entire twenty-four hours already, we have to admit you."

"But I don't have my luggage. I was about to go to lunch. I haven't eaten this morning. I'm starving." I could feel tears beginning to prick the corners of my eyes. Jeremy squeezed my hand.

The midwife smiled. "You need to go to the hospital, but if between here and the hospital, you happen to swing by your house and get your luggage or you happen to stop and get a sandwich, that's your business. You just need to be making your way to the hospital."

"Thank you."

Jeremy helped me off the table, and we made our way to the car. "We will go get lunch and then we'll take you to the hospital. It's going to be fine," he said.

"What about my bag?"

"I will go get your bag once they have you settled in. They just want to make sure everything is going okay." Anxiety crept in despite his comforting words.

We got in the car to go meet Melis's brother Bryan for lunch at our favorite Ham 'n Goodys, where the tears broke loose.

"I'm not in pain. I'm going to get there, and it's going to slow my labor down because I'm not ready. They're going to hook me up to things."

This is not the way I had planned it. I was not looking forward to being poked and prodded, loaded up with pain meds. Jeremy, who was calm and logical, comforted me again.

"It's going to be okay."

I was not calm and logical. I was devastated. I knew I wasn't ready. I knew if I got to the hospital significantly earlier than I needed to, they would want to get things going. They would give me drugs and take all of the naturalness out of the process. I wiped my eyes and tried to control my tears as we went into the restaurant.

An hour later, I was lying in the hospital bed, with a fetal monitor around my belly. I was one centimeter dilated and Melis was at my side. At least one thing was going as planned. I wanted Jeremy and Melis with me when the baby was born, but I had called and told Melis, "Don't worry about coming down right away. It's going to be a while."

In true Melis fashion she was there right when I needed her, the best distraction ever. She made me laugh, and her presence calmed some of my anxiety.

"You didn't have to come so soon. You might be hanging out for a while."

"I don't care," Melis said.

I was glad she didn't care. Sitting at the foot of the hospital bed, she took my feet in her hands and gave me a massage. If you have to go into labor, make sure to bring a friend who will rub your feet. We settled in for the long haul. Music was playing in the background. Jeremy and Melis took turns making me laugh. The hours ticked by. The nurse came in periodically to check me. Solomon's heartbeat was strong and steady. Even though this wasn't the birth I had planned, I couldn't help thinking, This baby is going to be so loved.

Five hours had passed. Nothing much was going on when Jeremy said, "I want to go down to the car and run to the house to get your bag."

We had come to the hospital directly from lunch. Our cute little house was only fifteen minutes away.

"You're good with Melis here," he said. "I'll just run and be back in thirty minutes."

"Yes, go. I will be fine."

The only medicine the nurses had convinced me to take was an antibiotic since my water had been broken so long at this point. A nurse had inserted a Foley bulb, a cervical catheter more or less, to manipulate the cervix to dilate without having to give me inducing medicine. I was okay with all of that. I was breathing through minor contractions. I was still at one centimeter. We could be in for a long night. Or at least that's what I was thinking when I told Jeremy to go. He had been gone all of five minutes when my stomach tightened in a way I had never felt before. Up until that moment, labor had been a walk in the park, more or less.

The contraction was incredibly uncomfortable—and long. As a first time mom, I didn't know contractions could be forty-five seconds to two minutes in duration. All I knew was that at some point they let up. But this contraction wasn't stopping. I shifted trying to find a comfortable position. Breathing in and out, doing my hypno-birthing techniques. The pain intensified. Melis could tell something was changing.

"Are you okay? Just breathe."

My stomach was so tight and hard I could hardly think straight. I started to feel like I was literally going out of my mind. The pain would not ease. Melis was at the foot of the bed, looking at the monitor. I was gripping the sheets trying to get a breath. The pain cut my voice. "Melis, something's wrong. This really hurts; this really, really hurts."

Her look of fear and concern mirrored my own. Suddenly nine people burst through the door. My midwife was there along with the shift nurse and a group of people I had never seen before. Three of them flipped me over on my side. A nurse emptied a syringe into my arm and got close to my face: "You are going to feel a little strange, but you will be okay."

My heart started racing.

"Just calm down," the nurse said. "You're going to be okay."

Someone checked to see if I was dilated. Fear surged in me like the medicine that was pouring into my veins. My own terror was reflected in the look on Melis's face.

"Where is her husband? Where is the father?"

"He just left to get her bag," Melis said.

"Call him. Tell him he has to come back!"

With that, someone slipped an oxygen mask over my face.

Melis called Jeremy. I heard the concern in her voice.

"Jeremy, you need to head back to the hospital. Well, they just put an oxygen mask on her so you can't talk to her." She looked at me. "He's on his way."

Thoughts were flooding my mind. What's going on? What aren't they telling us? I knew something was wrong. I could tell the medical team was trying to keep me from being scared but I was terrified. Finally, my body began to respond to the medication. My heart rate slowed, and the doctor finally had something to say.

"There, there. Now I can tell you. You were having basically an eight-minute contraction, and what we gave you is made to stop labor. We just hope it returns. We aren't sure why that happened, and we're hopeful it won't happen again."

The prolonged contraction had been restricting oxygen to the baby. Since I wasn't dilated, the contraction couldn't help push the baby out. It was just squeezing the life out of him.

In laymen's terms, a normal contraction is like a bear hug that manipulates the baby down through the birthing canal. But my baby couldn't move forward. He was stuck. While the contraction was taking place, his 151 beats per minute heart rate dropped to thirty-one beats per minute, triggering an alarm at the nurse's station. The doctor was explaining this to me when Jeremy finally arrived. I was crying. Melis was crying. Jeremy wrapped me in his arms. *What was going to happen to this baby we already loved so much?* I could not have cared less about my suffering. I just wanted them to save my baby.

A few hours later, it happened again. The panic. The medication. The heart rate dropping. Because we knew what was going on this time, it scared us even more.

At 4:00 a.m. it happened a third time, and I was still only one centimeter. They had begun discussing a C-section. All my carefully laid birthing plans were crumbling around me. I began to sob behind my oxygen mask, but there was something I needed to say.

"I can do this. If they will just let me try, I know I can have this baby naturally."

My midwife placed a comforting hand on my arm, "I know you can, Tiffany, but for some reason, your baby can't. I'm not going to risk that anymore."

As they wheeled me into the operating room, my body produced yet another elongated contraction. The only thing that would stop the contractions was the medicine being injected into my arm. Jeremy barely got into the operating room before they had me prepped, and via C-section, pulled out sweet, precious, healthy six pounds six ounces, nineteen-inches-long Solomon Fury Lee at 6:02 a.m.

I only saw Solomon for a moment before he was whisked away to the neonatal intensive care unit. I didn't see him again for almost three and a half hours. He had ingested meconium, or infant feces, and experienced stress so they had to clear his lungs and monitor him before returning him to me.

In all of this chaos, there was this huge comfort knowing that Melis and other wonderful family and friends were there in the waiting room.

Praying. Hoping. Seeing me in such unexplainable pain, however, had completely rattled Jeremy. It had also bonded him to me even more. He wanted to be with me. Yet, as a new mom, I wanted him to be with Solomon.

"I'll be okay," I told Jeremy. "Please promise me you'll stay with Solomon."

Melis had been watching over Solomon through the nursery window so Jeremy could sneak back to check on me. My mom was there, too, swapping out shifts on the baby vigil. They each took turns checking on Solomon and checking on me until we were given the clear.

Solomon had to be monitored for those first three and a half hours outside the womb. And I am not ashamed to admit, I started to get a little impatient with the situation. It's amazing how quickly you will do anything for someone you hardly know, yet already love so much. Before I had even locked eyes with this little boy, I had already told a doctor to do whatever it took to get him out safe.

Finally a little cradle rolled into my hospital room with Solomon Fury Lee. He was the most incredible thing I had ever seen in all of my life. His little lips puckered and his fingers bent back as he stretched and yawned and latched right on. We were in love. Uncontrollably, undeniably in love. He was our best collaboration by far.

All we could do was cry. And pray. And kiss him. And with great fanfare and the wildness of his birth, we were ushered into a new season. A season of joy and grace. Of chaos and unpredictability. Parenthood.

Nineteen months later, we welcomed—with great surprise—our sweet, big-eyed, adventurous, amazing Oliver Canon Lee, and twenty short months after that, a sister—our Sissy, as we like to call her—our precious Clementine Fire Lee.

We were full of love for these babies, full of thanksgiving for three beautiful, healthy children in less than four years.

We were also completely sleep deprived: I had three babies in diapers at once. Three babies needing help with most everything. Three babies, napping. Three more reasons to miss a shower and forget to eat.

Three more reasons to live life to its fullest. All things Plumb took a backseat to breast-feeding, wellness checkups, and potty training. Life had just gotten a whole lot crazier. We were in survival mode. We were hoping the odds were in our favor.

# Chapter 17
## Motherhood Unplugged

I HAVE BEEN INVITED to speak to various different groups over the years. One of the groups I have loved connecting with is MOPS, a support group for mothers of preschoolers. I get these women. They are beautiful, creative, and loving . . . and tired. Beyond tired. Mothers of preschoolers need an extra dose of love as it is being sucked out of them at an amazing rate. I have a strong bond with these women.

Melodi Leih was a part of inviting me to perform for a MOPS gathering when Clementine was all of nine weeks old. So when they experienced me leaking breast milk while I was on stage, they knew I was one of them. These are my people: The sleep-deprived ones with the crazy look in their eyes.

I have always wanted to be real and transparent with people when I meet them. Melis says that when you meet me, what you see is what you get. Good or bad, this is true. There is not a lot of sugar coating with me. I am who I am, a real woman with real hopes and real dreams and real stretch marks. And motherhood took me to a whole new level.

There is a perception about Christian artists that somehow we have a different way of dealing with life. That we have the inside track on figuring out how to follow Jesus or somehow know how to navigate the struggles of real living with more grace than your average person. This couldn't be further from the truth.

In almost every radio interview I give, one of the main questions I am asked is, "How do you balance being a wife, a mom, a performer, and songwriter?" And my answer every time is the same: "I don't."

And I don't. I try. I strive to find balance. I pray that God will give me the ability to sing, write songs, and connect with my audience. I long to find time to both soak in His word and love my kids and Jeremy Lee like mad—and still find time for a cup of hot tea with my girlfriends. For me, balance isn't a lifestyle. It is a daily challenge. Sometimes I hit it out of the park. I walk away from a day with a prayer of thanksgiving on my lips and contentment in my heart, knowing that I have gotten done what needs to be accomplished with grace. Other days, more often than not, it's a complete bomb, and all I can do is gather myself up and say, "Tomorrow is a new day." As my very wise sister-in-law, Daveta, always says, "His mercies are new every morning, Tif." I thank God for those fresh starts. Not so much the morning part, but definitely the fresh starts.

Balance is elusive. And what felt balanced last week may not feel balanced this week. I have always had high expectations about what I should be able to accomplish in a day. Those expectations tend to lead to disappointment. So I am learning. With so many different people and obligations pulling at me, it is an hour-by-hour quest just to be authentic and caring and still keep the kitchen floor free of ants. (Maybe it's a Tennessee thing, but geez Louise, those ants!)

Most often, I'm able to keep the kitchen floor clean because I have someone who works with me once a week that comes in to deep clean. That may not seem like a big deal to you. Maybe you have always had someone mop your floor. But it was a big deal for me to make that decision. My mom had always mopped her own floor. And my mother-in-law had always mopped her floor. In fact, they both still do. In my mind, now that I was a mom, I should be able to manage my family and bake brownies for playdates and keep the floor sparkling. Hiring a housecleaner felt like admitting defeat in some way. Sometimes expectations die a slow and painful death.

Life with three little ones three years and younger was a three-ring circus. I had this idea of what being a mother should look like. My mom, the self-proclaimed Domestic Goddess, made it look easy. Both my mom and Jeremy's mom, had chosen to stay at home, focusing on raising their children. Both Jeremy and I grew up knowing that no matter what, there wasn't anything our moms wouldn't do for us. And there was a sense of stability in knowing that when we walked through the door after school our moms would be there with a hug and a snack and a reminder to get our homework done. I love that about both of them. In my mind, I wanted my kids to have that same kind of experience. I wanted to be the mom that took care of the house and put a scrumptious meal on the table at dinnertime. That is what I wanted.

There is something so beautiful about who my kids are, and I want to nurture that. To feel Clementine's warm little body nestled next to me in bed, rubbing my arm, her little breath (that never stinks) on my cheek, wrenches my heart. To sit with Solomon, curled up close on the couch, playing with his fingers while reading a book and watching his eyes light up at a discovery, makes my entire day. To grab Oliver in a hug and get one of his famous kisses, hearing his giggles overflow and fill the room, lights something in me. I want the world for my children and then some.

The problem was I didn't know how I could give my children the world when mine seemed to biweekly fall apart. My days were a fog of sleepless nights and various bodily fluids. I was awash in breast milk and spit up and dirty diapers. I was no longer an artist. It was becoming clear that I cleaned baby bottoms for a living. I don't know how many hours of those early years were spent changing diapers. I actually don't want to know. What I do know is any creativity I possessed was spent trying to navigate a path through the piles of tiny clothes and teething toys that filled our house.

Truth be told, I was getting by on sheer grit and a nightly snack of chocolate or black licorice. My house seemed like it was never clean. My body was never showered. Poor Jeremy Lee. My vision of my becoming Miss Susie Homemaker was shattering before my eyes.

Who we were as a couple was also shifting. Jeremy and I had always had a creative, spontaneous energy to our relationship. If we wanted to go to a new restaurant, we would jump in the car and go. If we wanted to invite twenty people over for a spur of the moment barbecue, we did it. If we wanted to work in the studio for an extra morning, noon, or night, we booked it. But in a very short period of time, that free-spirited life that we had both craved and enjoyed became a scheduled machine. We were ruled by the clock.

Nursing a baby whittles your whole day down to three-hour segments. Before we would have said, "Let's go see that new movie coming out." Now I'd say, "In one hour and seventeen minutes, he's going to need to eat." Or, "In two hours and sixteen minutes, she's going to take her nap." Nap times were sought-after moments of respite. Each nap was golden. Untouchable. We would tell people, "Oh, we're so laid-back and flexible and spontaneous. We are just a party in a box!" But in reality, there was very little flexibility in our lives. Our schedules revolved around nap times and feedings.

People often tell me, "It's so great that you took a hiatus when your kids were born and took time off from touring and making records." But in reality, I was still trying to be Plumb while being a mom. Jeremy came up with the idea for *Blink*, my lullaby album while I was pregnant with Oliver. I thought he was crazy but, like always, Jeremy knew that doing something creative would feed my soul.

In between the nausea and the heartburn, I recorded some of my favorite songs I have ever written. I love every lullaby, every note, every thought put into that record. The love I felt for my sweet baby, Solomon, and this new little life churning in my belly poured into each ballad. I was thrilled to be a mom. The love we felt for our kids was immeasurable and palpable. *Blink* was a hit. We were blessed. We weren't planning on having our kids so close together in age, but it's turned out to be one of our greatest blessings. With each pregnancy has come an awareness that life would never be the same again. Life is messy. And it was about to get messier.

By the time I had Clementine, every day was its own battle to make it until Jeremy got home from the office. He was busy working with his dad with their import business. I had a potty-training three-year-old, an adventurous eighteen-month-old, and a tiny infant in diapers. It was three against one, and they were winning. I was in survival mode. I didn't have a moment to think about what was happening with Plumb.

You can't go on tour while you are potty training a toddler, at least I couldn't. You can't record when you have three little ones with stomach flu. You can't song write with your friends when you are breast-feeding on a three-hour cycle (pumping breast milk is the party foul of the universe). You can't do a photo shoot when you have an extra fifteen pounds hanging about your middle and your pants won't zip up. My life had flip-flopped. The things that brought me joy were shifting. And the things that brought me peace, well, I was having trouble finding any peace. I was just trying to breathe.

Jeremy saw me floundering and kept trying to offer me a lifeline. He knew that I was missing the creativity that fueled me. And he was missing the part of me that was creative, too. He would tell me, "Let's get a babysitter so you can record," or "Let's get someone to come be with the kids in the afternoon so you can get a coffee with Melis," or "Let's have Solomon go to Mom's Day Out so you can just have the two little ones for one morning a week." But I couldn't see the wisdom in this. To me, that would be shirking my duty as a mom.

I had no recollection of my mom ever needing a babysitter. She hadn't put me in a Mom's Day Out program. I never went to preschool. She kept both my older brother and me home until kindergarten. She had done it all. I wanted to do it all, too. I wanted to be the kind of mom that she was to me. The problem with that is that I am not my mom. I may act just like her sometimes talking with my hands and sound just like her at times, too, but we are two very different people. No one else expected me to be her. But I did. My expectation of who

I should be as a mother and the reality of who I was as a mother were miles apart. Oceans apart. I was drowning in a sea of failed expectations, with no clue what to do about it.

I knew that I was not a super domestic mom, but if I had my way I was going to die trying. I felt like I had a clear picture of what a mom should be: A good mom took care of her kids one hundred percent of the time. A good mom didn't need extra help to accomplish what needed to be done because she managed her time well.

So that's what I wanted. I wanted to have a clean house, three content babies, and a scrumptious dinner on the table when Jeremy walked in the door from work. I had this June Cleaver mom-in-an-apron expectation for myself. I even bought an apron. I love aprons, but at my core, I am not an apron-kind of girl. I couldn't admit that.

With my messy house, my manic scheduling, and my crumbling expectations, I was losing myself. Every day, my kids and Jeremy Lee were getting less of me. And it wasn't getting any better.

# Chapter 18
## Slow Chaos

ALL OF MY LIFE I HAVE thought of myself as an extrovert because I'm a talker and I do well in a room full of people. I can sing my heart out in front of thousands and I love being the comic relief in a group of friends. But I have learned, in reality, I am an introvert. I think my pride kept me from admitting this to myself for a long time. But Melis brought the truth to my attention with one telling observation: "I feel like I am going to kill someone if I don't work friend-time in or if I'm not around people. But you feel like you're going to kill somebody if you don't get away from all those people. I think it's important for you to be honest with yourself that you are actually refueled by that time to yourself. It's okay. Just admit it. That way, those around you who love you the most will be less disappointed with you if you can just be honest with yourself."

Ouch. They were the words of a good friend, though. When I am on the road, I am surrounded by people 24/7. When I get home, what I long for is a long hot bath, a good cup of tea, and sleep. Sleep is my favorite.

My perfect day of recharging after being on tour would be to arrive home around 10:00 a.m. after getting at least a solid nine hours of sleep on the bus. I would hop off and go straight to a massage followed by a piping hot cup of Refresh Tazo tea with honey from Starbucks. Jeremy would text me saying the kids were having a sleepover with their grandparents and having a blast. I would come home to an empty house to do laundry and organize every closet, drawer, and cabinet. Organizing is my language of love. A clean house orders my universe. I would catch a movie with Melis, eat some dinner I didn't have to make on a date with my hubby, and nibble some chocolate. After a relaxing bath, I would climb into a bed with fresh sheets and another cup of hot tea and check any e-mails or social media posts before falling into a blissful sleep without an alarm set. The kids would come home the next morning to a refreshed mom, a clean house, and a shiny new day. Perfection.

Now you should also know that in the real world of Tiffany Lee, absolutely positively none of that happens. Because life is life. It's crazy and messy and full to the brim with lovely children and hampers full of dirty clothes, and when I get off the tour bus, I jump straight back into that beautiful mess.

When I was pregnant with Clementine, I was already deep in the trenches of mommyhood. Besides my two little boys, I had severe anemia during my pregnancy with her—all while trying to sell our house. It didn't help that to sell a house you have to keep it "show ready." Ugh. It was difficult to see a whole lot of beauty in the mess.

This period of time began my slow downward spiral. I was experiencing a wild mix of emotions. The anemia had left me super lethargic and very grumpy. At the same time, I was still excited and anxious for Clementine to be born.

Our little cottage on Bluefield Avenue was also bursting at the seams. We decided to purchase a giant home about thirty-five minutes from our old neighborhood. It would have tons of space for our three little ones and a bigger backyard. It seemed like a great trade-off for living close to friends. It was a decision we would soon come to regret.

In reality, the move left me feeling isolated and anxious and it left us house-poor. We had sunk all of our money into the house with hardly anything left to furnish or decorate it. In a different season of life we might have thought, Maybe we should think about this a little more, maybe we can last another year in our cozy little house. But we were caught up in a whirlwind of baby wipes and hormones. Or at least I was.

We moved ten days before Clementine was born. Boxes were piled everywhere, and my once close-knit community was now miles away. Melis still came by to hang out and play with the boys while I nursed Clementine, but the daily running in and out of each other's lives slowed. She wasn't able to just pop over when she wanted to like in the past. I was also missing out on girls' night with my friends.

We were stretched to the limit financially. Some income was coming in from my publishing and radio play, but I wasn't touring or recording very much. In this industry, it always seems like you have to spend money to make money. Jeremy was managing me along with running our publishing company and holding down the import business with his dad. My main job was keeping the children alive. I was alone at the house with a three-year-old, an eighteen-month-old, and an infant. For a person who craves solitude, I was seeing very little alone time. And I was changing.

I was no longer the same confident rock star that Jeremy had married. I no longer felt comfortable in my own skin. I have always been a tiny five-foot, two-inches. Jeremy had once told me when we were dating, "I love how you fit perfectly underneath my chin."

Now I didn't recognize myself: Mentally, physically, or emotionally. My tiny frame was weighed down under baby flab. I didn't like my hair. Normally pretty light hearted and upbeat, I was now frazzled and cranky. Looking back, I can see that I had postpartum depression.

I have always thought people who were depressed stayed in bed in their pajamas all day crying. I wasn't doing that. I was going a mile a minute with my babies. I couldn't stop to breathe. But I also knew if someone had given me a "stay in bed all day" option, I would have taken it. I hadn't been diagnosed with attention deficit disorder yet, but the daily chaos of three little ones led to me being more disorganized, more unfocused, and more forgetful than ever. I was exhausted. I didn't feel beautiful. I was emotionally cutoff from my friends. My creative juices were drained. My sex drive was nonexistent. My love of life was seeping out of me, one drop at a time. I didn't know who I was anymore. But I loved my babies. I knew that much. I was crazy, stupid, nuts about my babies. Still am.

Jeremy was experiencing his own struggles. During my pregnancy with Clementine, he hadn't been sure what to do with me. I was difficult to live with. I was unmotivated and I was emotional. He knew I was having trouble coping but I wouldn't take any of his suggestions—whether it was getting a more consistent helper or getting out of the house to do something creative. We had always been super open about how we were feeling about things with each other, but in my present state he didn't feel like he could say, "Hey, you might consider maybe getting on medicine because you actually seem depressed sometimes, and you just don't realize it." He didn't feel like he could say, "I am stressed out, and it doesn't help when I come home and you are stressed out." He certainly didn't feel like he could say, "I am starting to feel disconnected from you." These are things you don't say to your pregnant anemic wife. But you probably should.

So instead of sharing this sense of disconnect with me—instead of telling me he was having a hard time being open and honest with me or that he felt the weight of the world on his shoulders—he kept quiet. And in his usual gregarious and entrepreneurial way, he made himself busy. He started to fill the space between us with activities, constantly suggesting, "Let's do this!" and "Let's go here!" and "Let's buy this." He was living life with an "eventually this season will pass" kind of attitude, as in, "eventually my wife will feel better about herself again and eventually the kids will get a little older and eventually the money will start to come back in. Eventually." Well, sometimes eventually is really, really far away. We were in that place of upheaval for a long while. And the months became years.

Sometimes life goes by in a flash. During this time of stress and growth and change I still felt connected to my husband. I still felt that we were bulletproof. I knew life was crazy; I just figured we had made it through so much together, this was just one more season. One more bad spell to endure. Everyone has a crazy life when they have little children. Everyone struggles with paying the bills every once in a while. But you stick together. You make it. In my mind, we were the unbeatable team, Tiffany and Jeremy. We were surviving and soon we would be thriving again. The kids were growing. The number of diapers we were changing was finally diminishing. Potty training had commenced. We were looking into schools for Solomon, and soon I would only have two little ones at home. Like I said, sometimes life goes by in a flash.

Jeremy was deeply invested in finding a good school for Solomon. After a ton of research, the only type of school that stood out to us was Montessori, but there were no Montessori schools in our area. The public schools that Solomon could attend were hit or miss as far as quality. We wanted him to have a creative learning experience in a place he could thrive. One day Jeremy came to me with an idea: "Tif, what if we start a school? We could offer something in our neighborhood that Solomon would love and that would be great for other families as well."

At the time we had just received a big publishing check. *What better way could we spend it?* We decided to jump in with both feet, Montessori or bust.

We met with educators and boards and eventually leased a building, bought all the supplies, hired a complete staff, and provided specialized training in the Montessori method for them. Jeremy was completely invested in every aspect of getting the school off the ground. I was completely supportive, but I felt like it was more his project than mine. I was immersed in our life at home. There were days that I didn't give the school a second thought, but my husband was carrying it with him constantly.

Anyone who has ever started anything from scratch knows what an enormous undertaking it can be. All the financial decisions, all the staffing decisions, all the facility decisions fell to Jeremy. The first few years of any new business are tenuous. Even though this was exciting and filling Jeremy's need to be hands-on, the responsibility was enormous. With all the emotional upheaval I was dealing with, he didn't feel I could handle the stress of the school. Unconsciously, he was separating himself from me in this area. Not because he didn't love me or value my opinion, but in an attempt to protect me. He didn't want to add to the daily stress that I already felt. What he didn't realize was in trying to protect me from the stress he was left alone carrying all of it, day in and day out.

Without recognizing it or asking for it, we were soon completely and totally overwhelmed. On the surface we looked like we were the family to be. We went on fun trips and had barbecues with our friends. We went to church on Sunday and had a business we could be proud of. We had it all going for us with our big house, our exciting careers, our beautiful children, and our thriving school. But just beneath the surface, not so much.

Jeremy was becoming an island, taking everything on his own shoulders, keeping his real thoughts and needs to himself. And me, well, I was clinging to this good life by my fingertips. I thought, if we could just make it a few more years, everything would be okay. The problem was we didn't have a few more years. The beautiful wild life we had built together was about to come crashing down around our ears.

# Chapter 19
## Bruised & Broken

I AM KNOWN FOR LEAVING long voice-mail messages. My friends make fun of the fact that what I need to say cannot be contained in a single message. Sometimes it takes three messages to get my full thought across. I have tried to explain that if I don't actually tell them what I am thinking about right at that exact moment, the thought will disappear into the ether of my mind, never to be seen or heard of again.

My good friend Bethany once told me she returned home one night from a horrible day at work feeling awful. When she checked the answering machine, there were four messages. They were all from me—made one right after the other. I was telling her how much I loved her and missed her and how I wanted to spend time with her. It was exactly what she needed that night: Four messages worth of love. I love that story.

Jeremy and Melis, even Tara, are not so appreciative of my long message leaving. They have been known to delete my messages without even listening to them. They think a five-minute message is four-and-a-half minutes too long. They just call me back, and our conversation always goes something like this: "I missed your call, Tif."

"Well, did you listen to my message?"

"No, what did it say?"

"Well, I don't remember. That is why I left you a message in the first place—because I knew I wouldn't remember." My final words are usually relayed with a deep sense of frustration. My husband and friends are unperturbed.

"Well, when you remember, call me back."

So I have taken to texting. I think they appreciate this. They like that my texts are short and to the point and less than five-minutes long. I used to think texting was for quick notes, funny pictures, and reminders about tae kwon do lessons and groceries that needed to be picked up. But that all changed the day I read the text that turned my world inside out.

In 2011 stress had seeped into all areas of life for the Lee family. Early in the year, Jeremy had gone for his annual checkup and learned he had developed Type 2 diabetes. It blindsided him. The diagnosis meant medication, shots, and finger-pricking—another layer of to-dos on his already overloaded plate.

The import business with his dad was thriving, which had meant several trips to China and back for Jeremy. On the other hand, our school was struggling. We had started the school in 2010 with a three- to six-year-old classroom. In less than a year we had added a toddler class and a lower elementary class. Each classroom cost about twenty-five thousand dollars to set up. By trying to accommodate more students, we had placed ourselves in a precarious position financially.

School was due to start for the fall session in August, and it looked like we may not be able to able to open the doors. I could see the tension in Jeremy's face when he came home each night. Owning a school was no small thing. It was huge. We were finding out just how huge.

All three of our kids were also enrolled in the school. Solomon was in the lower elementary class by this time. Oliver was in the primary class, as was Clementine, a couple mornings a week.

The school had opened on a wing and a prayer. We were hoping the finances would stabilize throughout the year.

In some ways, the school had opened up the space in our home for me to breathe. With the kids thriving there, I was back in the studio, writing and recording the songs for my next album. I was finally seeing a light gleaming at the end of the baby tunnel. The creative me was coming to life again. The songs were flowing, which meant we had a huge collection of songs to pick from for the new album.

One of my favorites of the new songs was "Need You Now." It was a song I had written with my friends, Luke Sheets and Christa Wells, about my struggle with panic and anxiety attacks throughout my teenage years. It was a song that I felt went to the core of who I was.

All in all, things seemed to be coming together. I was excited to be working with Matt again, and we hired a new manager, Chris Bradstreet. With the school, the import business, and our publishing company, Jeremy was ready to let someone else manage me. And we both knew it would relieve some of the pressure he was feeling about having to manage every aspect of my career. It was a good place to be in life.

Or that was what I thought. Jeremy was having other thoughts. He was worn down by our crazy life over the last five years. Being a full-time manager, publisher, importer, school-owner, dad, and husband had left him feeling wrung out. Dealing with my emotional struggles and trying to motivate me to be creative had also drained him. Finding out he had diabetes was just icing on the crap cake.

My husband is an incredibly upbeat person. When you meet him, you can't help but be attracted to his open and easy personality. He is always smiling. Energetic and excitable, he is a people-magnet. But on a Tuesday in November of 2011, I noticed changes in him: Jeremy was angering more easily. Irritated and impatient, he wasn't acting like himself. I was concerned but didn't know what to do, so I called his doctor.

"Is there any way that a diabetic's behavior could be altered from his medication or lack thereof? Because my husband is not acting like someone I know lately," I told the doctor. "He's super grumpy, super critical, and really tired. He seems disconnected, and what little connection there is, it's just rude and impatient."

"Yes, blood sugar does affect your moods so he definitely needs to check his blood sugar regularly," the doctor confirmed, but he also cautioned me. "You can encourage him to take his medication, but he is a grown man. So don't nag him too much because sometimes that can make it worse." (Our sweet family doctor for years didn't know that it wasn't diabetes at all.)

At home, I watched Jeremy's behavior as the week went on. I put up with him being rude, critical, and impatient unlike anything I'd ever seen in him before. I told myself he had put up with a lot from me over the past few years, and I waited for a time to talk to him about his diabetes. I didn't want to push him, but I was concerned about him.

And then I came down with strep. Normally, in our house, Jeremy is more of a caretaker to me than I am to him. He is attentive and kind and nurturing whenever I am sick, constantly checking in on me. Me? I'm more of a ring-a-bell-if-you-need-me kind of girl with him. But as I lay in bed, trying not to cry from how much my throat hurt, I could hardly talk. I was miserable—and on my period, to make matters worse.

It was a Tuesday, and Jeremy was getting ready to leave for work. The kids were already at school. Jeremy walked in the bedroom and slammed my medication on the table, with a curt, "See you." No "Are you okay?" or "Can I get you anything before I leave?" or "I love you."

I whispered, "Can you get me some orange juice?" I could sense he was irritated with me. He returned with the orange juice without a word and left for work. He was annoyed but I wasn't sure why.

Later that morning, curled up in my blanket I pulled out my phone and texted him: *You are not your normal joyful self today. Is there something that I've done to make you upset? I know that I'm on my period and I have strep throat, so I'm probably not the most fun to be around this week. . . . But hopefully by next week I will be back to normal.*

A text shot back.
*I've been pretty frustrated lately.*
Thinking his frustration had something to do with work, I answered. *Really? With what?*
*With you.*

And there it was. *With me.* My phone dinged again.

*I cannot live like this for the next twenty years. I've thought about separating, but I know that neither one of us can be away from the kids.*

My heart began to pound in my throat; my face flushed with heat. Blinking back tears, I wrote back. *Is this a joke? Because it's not funny.*

*I wish I was joking.*

*You're scaring me.*

*I'm not meaning to scare you, but I've been frustrated for a while, and I just don't think I can live like this anymore.*

I was crying at this point. My hands were shaking. How was this happening? I texted him again. *Please call me.*

*I can't.*

*You're not able to talk right now?*

*I can't.*

*You can't talk right now, or you can't talk to me?*

*I can't talk to you.*

*Please call me immediately.*

Finally my phone rang. "Hello?"

Jeremy was really quiet.

"Hello?" I said again.

"Hey." His voice was hushed.

I tried to keep the panic out of my voice, "What is this?" More silence. "Jeremy, what is this? If this is a joke, it's a horrible prank, and if it's not a joke, you are terrifying me. . . . the way your text reads, it sound like you don't want to be married to me anymore, and we don't even joke like that much less talk like that."

"Well, that's exactly what it reads," he said.

I could barely breathe. I knew life had been crazy, and he was under a lot of stress but to me it was just a season. It wasn't a reason to end our marriage. For me this was coming completely out of left field. All I could think was, I wonder if he has stopped taking his medication.

This really can't be Jeremy that I am speaking to. I tried to sound calm. I didn't want to upset him further. "Well, we've got to talk about this."

"Well, tonight I'm busy. We'll just have to talk tomorrow."

His buddy Dodge was having a birthday party that night.

You don't expect to ask for a glass of orange juice and have your husband tell you he is thinking of leaving you. The next few days were a Twilight Zone. I didn't call Melis and tell her about the text. I didn't mention anything to my mom when she came over to watch the kids later that night while Jeremy was out. It would have made it too real.

This wasn't just a little fight. This wasn't a social media misunderstanding. This was a five-minute text exchange that threatened the foundation of my world. Jeremy wasn't talking to me, at least not about anything that mattered. There were no good-night kisses, which I chalked up to the strep. But even when he crawled in bed with me at night, his back was turned to me, a wall of silence split us down the middle.

By the time Thursday rolled around, I had begun to feel better. I texted my husband. *We need to talk.*

*I know tonight is our date night, but would you like to go have a night out with the girls?*

Each little word of that text from Jeremy hurt my heart. He didn't even want to do date night. My heart sunk, but I tried to rally. *Well, I love time with my girls, but I feel like based on what you said forty-eight hours ago in a text message, I think it's very important that we go out together and talk.*

*Okay, well, we can work that out. We can go to dinner somewhere and talk.*

I spent the day with my worries. My fears. And praying everything was going to be okay.

That night when I got in the car, Jeremy turned and asked me, "Well, what do you want to talk about?"

I was looking at his face, the face of this man I loved so much. And I was scared and hurt. What I wanted him to say was, Look, I was talking crazy the other day. I don't know what's wrong with me. I feel completely overwhelmed. But that didn't happen.

"You know," I said, "I really think you're the one that has the most to say because I'm completely caught off guard."

An incredulous look appeared on his face.

"You're really caught off guard by this?"

I flushed, feeling stupid, and said, "Uh, I am. I mean, I do know that I've been sick, and I've probably been grumpy this week, but I don't know that that merits a message like that."

We made our way inside Bonefish Grill. The smells coming from the kitchen were delicious, but I felt as if I were going to throw up. Conversations were happening all around us. But I was having a conversation that I never thought would happen in my lifetime.

Jeremy Lee looked across the table at me. His pupils were big and black. Any show of kindness or love that I usually saw mirrored in his eyes was gone, replaced by a look of contempt. He was thirty inches away from me. It could have been thirty feet.

"Well, let me tell you why I am frustrated," he said, and he proceeded to list all of the things that he didn't like about me.

He listed off eleven things in a row that he "hated" about me—from how self-centered I was to how I talked way too much. He said if he had to listen to one of my stories one more time, he would shoot himself. Each dislike he ticked off was like a physical blow. No one in the world knows me as well as Jeremy, and so, yes, there were bits and pieces of truth to some of what he was saying. But I felt he was using the opportunity to point out every weakness, every flaw that he had ever seen in me. It was painful to say the least.

I couldn't stop the tears pouring down my cheeks. And as I sat there and took it, I started to feel scared for him. I know Jeremy as well as he knows me, and this was not Jeremy Lee. My husband is gracious and forgiving. Something must be wrong with him, I thought. Jeremy must be going through something and he is not himself.

His words pummeled my heart, but I wiped my eyes, looked at him.

"I'm going to work on everything that you told me to work on," I said, "and I'm going to have a better attitude, and I'm sorry."

He leveled a stony stare at me from across the table.

"Well, that doesn't fix it."

"I have to start somewhere," I said as my voice cracked.

I leaned down and pulled a pen and paper out of my purse. I started writing down every complaint he had said about me.

"What are you doing?"

"I'm making a list."

"What are you going to do with it?"

"I don't know how long it will take me, but I'm going to work on this list for the rest of my life if I have to. I don't want to be someone that you don't want to be married to. I'll change." Tears slipped down the side of my nose dripping into my lap. "I'll work on me."

Nothing I was saying changed the look on his face.

"I don't know that that's even going to help."

"I think we need to go to counseling."

And then he made one final statement by way of a question, "Do you feel defeated?"

"Why?"

"You should." With that he stood and with a cynical tone said, "Yeah, let's go to counseling."

It most certainly didn't sound as if his heart was in it. I didn't know where his heart was. Somewhere in the chaos of the last five years, I had been losing little pieces of his heart and hadn't realized it. And in the last three days, he had managed to shatter mine.

I didn't even know who I was without Jeremy. Losing his love was like losing the blood that flowed through my veins. He was air and love and life to me. We struggled through some counseling sessions. He remained aloof around the house while I walked on eggshells trying not to upset what tenuous accord existed.

When I did look into his eyes, he wasn't the Jeremy Lee I knew, the man I married eleven years before. I didn't know what he was thinking. I didn't know all the reasons he was drifting away from me and even some that I did are still too painful to talk about. I didn't know who Jeremy had become but I knew this was not the man I had fallen in love with.

On December 27, 2011, Jeremy told me he was leaving me. And when he walked out our front door with his things to go and stay at a friend's, he took my soul with him. The world went black.

# Chapter 20
## Winter

ONE OF THE THINGS THAT I LOVE best about living in Nashville is the weather. I love the green smell of spring as the first flowers and leaf buds begin to show up. I love the heat of summer warming my skin and the sound of my kids shouting as they jump in the pool. I love the cool breezes of fall that ruffle the red and gold leaves of the trees. And I love winter. I love when it is so cold outside that it hurts and the only thing left to do is snuggle on the couch with a cup of cocoa and watch the snow flurries flit against the window.

Snow days are the best. They are a mandatory day in. Who doesn't love being told that they have to stay home and have fun? Snowball fights, snow angels, and old movies are the order of the day. The only thing I don't like about winter is the yard after the snow has melted when the trees are bare and the grass turns that dead brown color. Everything looks lifeless and shut down then. There is no hint of flowers or spring, just that gross brown slush that lines the streets. That is when winter makes me sad.

When Jeremy left the house two days after Christmas, it felt like that dead part of winter had taken up residence inside my soul. Life was cold and hard and ugly. Everything that was good about life had withered away.

How do you go on when the person you love most of all doesn't want you anymore? How do you breathe when all the air has been knocked out of your chest? How do you get out of bed when the worst thing you have ever imagined happening, save for something happening to your children, is your new reality?

I wanted to curl into a ball and go to sleep and not wake up until the nightmare was over. Jeremy's leaving didn't just impact our marriage. Our lives were so intertwined, so interwoven, that everything was changed. The school, our kids, our friendships, our families, Plumb—everything had to shift and separate and make space for the distance between us.

As for me, I still couldn't believe this was happening to us. I was so clueless. I hadn't seen what was coming until it smacked me in the face and left me reeling. But looking back, I should have. Our relationship was like a windshield. Pure and true and strong. But through the years, it had been getting a lot of dings, and those pointed little rocks of stress and busyness and miscommunication had chipped away at its strength. It looked good from far away. But up close, it was laced through with a network of tiny stress fractures, each one growing a little each year until it finally shattered all at once. The weeks following the breakup of our marriage left me trying to pick up the sharp-edged pieces to a puzzle that no longer fit together.

Solomon was almost seven. Oliver was newly five. Clementine was three and a half. As much as we could, we shielded our kids from what was going on, telling them Daddy was staying at Grandma and Grandpa's because he was working on a project.

I was hoping that project was us. I was praying it was. I was hoping that while he was living with his mom and dad he would realize he couldn't live without us, without the children and me. Mostly, that he couldn't live without me. Because I knew I didn't want to live without him. He was the love of my life. Even though I was so hurt, I still loved him. The kids needed their daddy. I needed my husband. We needed to be a family. I couldn't see how anything else could work.

When I kissed the kids good night and they asked me who I loved the most I always answered, "Daddy. I love Daddy the most." I never changed that answer, but I waited to cry until I could put my bedroom door, the bathroom door, and then the toilet door between us. Three closed doors to block the sound of my broken heart. Hoping even as I gave in to the tears that they were asleep. Sometimes I slept on the floor next to their beds or climbed in bed next to my oldest in an effort to draw warmth and comfort from Solomon who was now the "man of the house."

Despite our best efforts, Solomon, our old soul, could sense the distress in our home. His behavior began to regress; there were accidents and several bouts of throwing up. He had never seen Jeremy and I remain apart for so long. After three weeks, our counselor suggested that Jeremy move back in, at least temporarily. So in late January, Jeremy moved into the guest room.

I don't know if it was worse having him live far away or living at home. I was living with a stranger. Having him near, sucked the joy out of me. He was home just long enough for the kids to see him head to the shower and tuck them in, thinking Daddy was home for the night. They had no idea Daddy went straight to bed in the guest room. And Mommy slept alone in her oversized master bedroom, more alone than ever before.

The only true thing of beauty during this winter was how our community held us up. All those friends that had been with us since our dating days, rallied around us. Later we would find out that two days after he left me, forty of our closest friends gathered in the chapel we were married in to pray for us. They held us up in prayer, then in the weeks and months ahead held us up physically with calls, food, babysitting, and more prayers.

Even though our friends were heartbroken about Jeremy's decision, they didn't leave him. And they certainly didn't stop loving him. They were able to see something most can't: That Jeremy's behavior wasn't Jeremy Lee. It was evil. So together they asked God to do what only He could do, overcome evil's stronghold on God's very own. They wanted our marriage to do more than just survive. They were praying for reconciliation and redemption. And then there was Melis.

Almost as heartbroken as I was, Melis didn't offer advice. She didn't tell me that Jeremy was a jerk. She loved us. Not me. Us. She loved Jeremy like the older brother she never had. She made a point of telling Jeremy that she loved him and was praying for him and that her role right now was best-served standing behind me and pushing me towards reconciliation, while still loving and praying for him. She didn't choose sides but rather chose to help where she was most needed. And at that time, it was near me.

She didn't tell me everything would work out or that Jeremy and I were going to get back together. Instead she said, "Tif, no matter what happens, because of Jesus, ultimately you're going to be okay." She spoke hope into my life when I didn't know where else to look for it. Newly married herself, she and her husband must have prayed a thousand prayers on our behalf. I was wounded, scared, and uncertain of the future. But whatever was going to happen, I knew that I wasn't going to face it alone.

I also turned to my listeners and fans for support. Without sharing any actual details on my Facebook page, I let them know I was hurting and going through an incredibly difficult time, and I asked them often to pray for me. Thousands of listeners responded with words of hope and encouragement—the same people who had so often approached me after concerts and said, "Your song has made a difference in my life" or "Thank you for the words you sing; it's exactly what I'm going through."

Now the tables had turned. My listeners were lifting me up with their words. They were offering me their hope to lean into.

I filled my home with Christian music. Something I hadn't done in quite some time. I love the artistry and styling of a lot of different music. And I had been prideful. Thinking I was too cool for Christian music. That somehow I was better than it. But I became desperate to fill my mind with music offering hope and strength.

I had Christian radio on 24/7 in every room of the house. I played it in the car. I played it while I was in the shower. I left it on at night. Still do. I wanted those truths seeping into my bones, filling the air of my home, and chasing away the fear and doubt that hovered in the wings of my mind. Songs laced with hope and healing were building up my spirit: "Our Hope is in You" by Aaron Shust, "Always Forever" by Phil Wickam, "Stronger" by Mandisa, "Strong Enough" by Matthew West, "Lead Me" by Sanctus Real, "Thrive" by Switchfoot, and "I Need a Miracle" by Third Day.

I was grounding myself in the truth. Work on my own album had been set aside until we could figure out what was going to happen with Jeremy and me. But my song "Need You Now" had taken on a different meaning for me. I had never needed God like I needed Him in that moment. Losing Jeremy Lee was worse than a truckload of panic attacks. The lyrics of my song were the embodiment of everything I was feeling and working through.

I didn't have a plan to win Jeremy back. I didn't have any idea of how to go about making him fall back in love with me. I didn't know how to act around him. I just knew that I wasn't done loving him. Even though his words and actions hurt me, I wasn't ready to give up.

I asked our friends to meet with him, to reason with him. I asked his parents to talk some sense into him. I kept orchestrating things and manipulating things to work it out to my liking. But in the few real discussions he and I had at the house, I couldn't hide my pain of being rejected. I would speak sarcastically to him about hard things happening at his work, saying, "I don't know, maybe if you wanted your wife, that wouldn't happen." He brushed me off.

His best friends and family were all preaching at him. Telling him that he needed to reconcile. Nothing got through to him. If anything, it all pushed him further away from me.

Jeremy Lee wanted nothing to do with me. All my manipulations failed. One day, in a moment of clarity, I realized there was nothing I could do or say that was going to save my marriage. I had to let Jeremy walk out the path he had chosen. I couldn't force him to be or do what I wanted. He needed to be able to make his own choices.

I was grief stricken. The Jeremy I knew was gone. He wasn't my husband anymore. But I couldn't do anything about that. My heart was breaking all over again at the thought of actually living life without him, but strangely, I felt a sense of release and a sense of peace when I made my decision. I was choosing to let go of Jeremy and fall back into the arms of the One who loved me most of all. I let go of my plans and prayed, "I love you Jesus. You are all I have now. And You are enough. I'm done. I'm done trying to play God."

When Jeremy left the guest room to go to his work the next day, I had coffee with my precious new friend Trisha. She had been through much of what I was going through. She gave me affirmation that I had to let go. That I was getting in the way. That I had to trust God to do what only He could do. Our marriage and family therapist, who I am forever indebted to for her strength and wisdom and patience and confidence in the Holy Spirit, had said the same. Get out of God's way. You can't change him. But you can work on you. Pray for Him to intervene. And be honest with yourself. Be genuine in what you need to change. Not for Jeremy Lee. But for the God who created and loves you. So that you can be all He wants you to be no matter what Jeremy decides.

So I got to work. I began by taking everything that was Jeremy's and piling it out by the garage. I wasn't doing it out of hate. I was giving Jeremy what he wanted and ultimately what he needed. I was letting go of him. Giving him a life free of me. When he got home, he must have seen the pile of his stuff because he knocked instead of just coming in.

"Tif, what's going on?"

I spoke to him through the locked door. "I'm letting you go. I'm not going to file for divorce. If you want to divorce me, you're going to have to do that. But do what you've got to do. And we'll make a plan for how to behave for our children. Good-bye Jeremy Lee."

I didn't know how we were going to break the news to our kids or our friends and family, but I was done trying to stop Jeremy from leaving. The more I tried . . . the worse it got. So I let go.

The desperate longing to reconcile with Jeremy for the last three months had fallen away to be replaced with sadness: Sadness that I didn't know him. Sadness that he was choosing to walk away from our marriage. Sadness that my love was changing. But oddly enough, I also felt a sense of relief. I wasn't in control of what was going to happen anymore. That was between God and Jeremy. And there was Kay Warren's *Choosing Joy*, again, I had to choose it. I had to have the confidence that the God of the universe loved me and would never leave me. That no matter how bleak it appeared, God was in control. And He was present.

In February, I met with my label and my manager. We talked about what the future would look like for Plumb since it looked like divorce was in my future. I shared with them, "I gave Jeremy all of his stuff. I don't see a way out of this. I have always said there is always hope, but I can't see it."

I also met with a lawyer to find out what I should be prepared for if Jeremy filed for divorce. Jeremy remained in a very dark place and his distant attitude hadn't changed. I needed to start thinking about the future in a different way. Relinquishing my rights to Jeremy as his wife was changing me. I didn't realize it then but I was finally getting out of God's way.

It was in these moments of letting go, of not fighting Jeremy in his decision to walk away, that I finally, for what I now know as the real first time, fell in love with Jesus more than Jeremy Lee. I fell into Him. I melted into Him, and rested there. I stopped trying to make things happen and started leaning into the truth that even if everything fell apart, Jesus remained. I was safe in His care. In that moment of release, it was like Jesus put His arm around me to help change me and grow me and then with His other arm, He started working on Jeremy.

Jeremy was in a battle for his life within himself. He was desperate. He was alone. He was stuck in a place of confusion. And when I told him that I was done trying to keep him, it was as if a slow light dawned on his darkness. One of my favorite stories about winter takes place in the *Chronicles of Narnia* by C.S. Lewis. The ice from the wicked snow queen is beginning to melt. Green buds are sprouting on bare tree branches, and the Beaver tells the children, with a grin and a huge amount of hope, "Aslan is on the move."

I didn't know it then but things were shifting in Jeremy. God was at work, doing only what He could do. Our winter was about to give way to an unexpected spring. Hope was about to show up.

# Chapter 21

## Healing

I THINK I HAVE THE THREE best children in the world. Of course, I am completely unbiased. Like most parents, Jeremy and I love our kids to the moon and back. They surprise us, they make us laugh, and, of course, they make us crazy. But one of the coolest things about having kids is seeing how different parts of their personalities are interesting combos of our personalities. They have some traits that are like me, different traits that are like Jeremy, different qualities that remind us of our family members, and then some qualities that are uniquely their own.

Solomon, as I mentioned before, is wise beyond his years. He is a thinker, an observer. He isn't easily swayed or influenced by other kids. He is completely his own man. He can struggle, much like his mother, with staying focused and self-motivated, but he is generally a calm, content, and kind little boy. He has a great sense of humor and a strength of character that was evident even as a toddler. And he is an amazing big brother. I love how he loves. It's never for show, so what you see with him is real.

I wrote "In My Arms" about Solomon. I remember looking down at his sweet baby face as I rocked him and feeling that he fit perfectly in my arms. He was safe and secure with me and that made me feel safe and secure. But I also had a sense that even as a baby, I had to entrust him to the arms of God. I wouldn't be able to hold him forever. I can't protect him forever. But God can take care of this precious boy in a way I never can. I find him inspiring. He's thoughtful. He's smart. And his hugs are magical. They have healing powers. As he grows I can already see a light in him, a hunger to see what God is going to use him to do.

Oliver is Mr. Adventure, a party waiting to happen. He's pure happiness. He's entertaining. He brings joy to every room he enters. He's fun and full of energy. He sees life as a huge adventure and every day he wants to take a bite out of it. I sometimes have felt undeserving that God gave me the gift of allowing me to be his mother.

Oliver has a very tender and sensitive heart. One day he told me, "Mom, when you get really, really, really, really, really, really old, I will take care of you." I squeezed him and said, "Thank you, buddy."

He looked up at me with his big blue eyes just like his daddy's and said, "I'll even wipe your bottom." Now that is love.

This boy is like candy to me. I wrote "Don't Deserve You" about him. In the song I sing, "Your heart is golden. How am I the one that you've chosen to love? I still can't believe you're right next to me after all that I've done." I meant every word. Oliver is one of the most spectacular people I've ever met in my life; he's taught me more about unconditional love than almost anyone I've ever known. (Can you tell I have a little crush on both my boys?)

My daughter Clementine is for better or for worse just like me. But better. She isn't prissy. She isn't a tomboy. She's somewhere in-between, just like me. She isn't afraid of the mud and yet she is a girl's girl, just like me. She loves to dance and take gymnastics and piano, just like I did. She is enthralled by makeup and nail polish and accessories, just as I was. She has a love affair with every color of the rainbow, and she loves to get dressed up and put fun outfits together. Again, ditto. Clementine loves to write notes, which is where my mom clearly recalls my writing began. She is more excited about new shoes than candy any day. She can be stubborn like her daddy, and I see an unwavering strength in her because of that. She is super funny, like, clever funny. I love that about her. And she is very affectionate. She loves nothing more than to rub my bare arm when she feels tired or nervous or sad. More like her daddy, Clementine is a helper. Very independent and secure in herself, she is smart and compassionate. When someone is hurt or sick, she wants them to be better and wants to help to make that so. I love that my daughter feels for other people. That is a beautiful thing.

Long before Clementine arrived on the scene, I had thought about what it would be like to have a daughter of my own. Even when I was in high school, some of my decisions were influenced by the thought of having a daughter someday. There were times that I did not do certain things because I would think, I would never want to have to tell my daughter that I did that. I want to be the type of woman my daughter can be proud of and look up to. Long before I ever held my daughter, the idea of her saved me from a lot of poor choices and gave me the courage to take risks that were necessary to grow. I am so thankful that Clementine is mine. I have told her that I will always fight for her, even if I have to fight *her*. And sometimes I do. And it's always worth it.

Yes, Jeremy and I are blessed with some great kiddos. While we were separated, I tried to protect them from the worse of it, especially from being afraid. I was trying to protect them from being sad. I was trying to protect them from having insecurities. I was trying to protect them from feeling anxious. I was trying to protect them in every way. But they will never know how much trying to protect them kept me going, kept me living and breathing. Had I not had them to protect who knows where I'd be. Their sweetness, their needs, their little fights, their schedules, their meals kept me focused on being a mom. Their need for me gave me strength and held me in place when everything else around me was shifting.

When Jeremy moved out for the second and final time, he moved in with his parents. And he missed our kids. He is a very hands-on dad. He was missing out on being with them. In walking away from me, he walked away from us as a family, and it weighed on him. He began calling to see if he could come see the kids. He needed them and they needed him. When he would come over I would leave to run errands or hang out with Melis or go see a movie. I wanted the kids to be with their dad, but I didn't hang around. I gave Jeremy his space. I was letting God do what He needed to do in Jeremy Lee. And I was asking Him to do what He needed to do in me to change and heal me, too.

When I had told Jeremy that I was done trying to make him stay, something began changing in his heart. And something changed in mine. Instead of living in a place of hopelessness as the rejected wife, I could step out of those emotions now and see Jeremy not as a husband but as a person. And in that place, I was finding this inexplicable grace to forgive him, as I would want him to forgive me.

Our campus pastor Justin once said that "forgiveness may not always heal the relationship but it does heal your heart." Withholding forgiveness causes you to suffer more. Withholding forgiveness is like cancer, it kills you from the inside out. I'd never in my lifetime been as challenged to forgive someone as I was when Jeremy left me.

I remember telling Jeremy, tears running down my face, "Jesus had the power to take Himself off of the cross, but He stayed. He knew what I was going to do. Still, He loved me enough to endure the cross. I want to love like that. So, I am choosing to stay and forgive, because I have never wanted to love like Jesus more in my life."

I also made it clear to Jeremy that if he still chose to leave, it was his choice. I only knew that I would be able to sleep better at night and hold my head higher knowing that I was willing to do whatever it took to save our marriage, and I would be able to look my children in the eyes with dignity. I became willing to change whatever I needed to change because I wanted to love like Jesus loved. And I wanted to do it for Him. Not Jeremy this time.

I realized I had made an idol out of my husband. For that, I had to take ownership—among a lot of other things for which I had to take ownership. I had fallen head over heals for the One who will never leave me, who will always be faithful, who will always protect, who will always provide, who will always forgive, who will always have the answer. That's who I'm in love with now. Having developed a romantic love for Jesus, I'm able to love others better.

It was a difficult thing to say, but I wanted to be able to say it and mean it: I wanted to be able to forgive Jeremy. And in letting my heart change, I was feeling something new. I was feeling compassion for Jeremy. After our conversation, I sent him a text a few days later: *I hope that if nothing else because of our history and the children we share together, maybe I can be your friend. Maybe I can help you get through this darkness you seem to be drowning in. Because if nothing else, you are the father to our three children and they deserve your best, and the person you are hurting the most right now is yourself.*

With that message, something broke free in Jeremy. He had walked away from our family and me. He had walked away from God. He had done things for which he wasn't proud. But he was discovering in the middle of this dark place God's enormous grace and forgiveness. God was chasing hard after Jeremy Lee. And I had to trust him with Him.

Meanwhile, Jeremy, by way of invitation from our close friend Ricky, was going to a new church called Cross Point in Nashville. Justin, the campus pastor there, took Jeremy under his wing and was able to love him exactly how he needed to be loved: Tough. On his first Sunday, the head pastor, Pete Wilson, welcomed everyone by saying "Good morning, welcome to Cross Point, where it's okay to not be okay. Here at Cross Point, everyone is welcome, nobody's perfect, and anything is possible." It was just the attitude Jeremy needed.

Jeremy told me later that when he received that text from me, "All the pressure came off to do the 'right thing.' All the pressure came off to love you. All the pressure came off to be someone that I've not been. And because all the pressure came off, on my own I actually wanted to do what was right. I hadn't cared about doing what was right for months. It was the first time since I left that I felt like I had the freedom to choose. No one was forcing me anymore. I suddenly had a desire to do everything I could to fight for my family and my marriage.

I may never get it back. There may not be any hope. But I'm going to die trying."

I didn't know any of this at the time, but I knew he was missing the kids, so when he asked one Sunday night what we were doing I told him.

"We're going to Five Points Pizza, why?"

"Can I join you?"

"Sure."

I didn't know how such an outing was going to work what with us being separated, but I knew that I wanted the kids to feel comfortable out with us together. I didn't want our children to feel like there was tension or anger between their parents. I was in a place of grace. When I walked into Five Points Pizza, Jeremy was already there at a table. The kids swarmed him, hugging him.

"I already ordered the pizza," he said.

We settled the kids into their seats. Their beverages were already at their places, and Jeremy had ordered root beer for me.

I was a little miffed that he had ordered mine. I thought, You don't even want me, so don't do something that shows how you know me, and order my favorite drink. When the server walked by, I flagged him over and ordered a Diet Dr. Pepper.

"Diet Dr. Pepper?" I heard Jeremy say.

I avoided eye contact with him. I didn't want him to know the ins and outs of who I was or what my favorite things were anymore. I was trying to create a distance between us of my own. I didn't look him in the eye for a while. I have always been able to tell how Jeremy was feeling by the look in his eyes, and for the last few months the only thing that his eyes had told me was that I was unwanted. I was tired of looking in the eyes of a stranger.

The pizza arrived at the table piping hot, and we both helped the kids get their pieces. With the kids distracted by garlic knots and cheese pizza, I finally looked up and caught Jeremy's eye. I was stunned. He was noticeably different. I couldn't help blurting out, "It's you!" I was looking into the eyes of the man I had always loved and the one who had always loved me back. He was there. Jeremy just kept looking at me, not saying anything.

"Hi," I said.

"Hi," he said, his eyes growing misty.

"It's you."

"Yes, it's me."

His eyes filled with tears; my eyes filled with tears. *What was going on?*

"Let's just enjoy our pizza," Jeremy suggested. "I sent you an e-mail to read when you get home."

And so we did. We finished our pizza, while I stole looks at him across the table when I thought he wasn't looking. *What was my Jeremy Lee doing back? What was he thinking? What did his e-mail say?* In that one long mutual look, I had seen a true drop of hope. But as I have said before, One drop of hope can lead to an ocean overflowing with it.

When I got home, I put the kids to bed. I felt a little sweaty, and I felt the first excitement I had felt since Jeremy had left me. I prayed with the kids and kissed them and grabbed my laptop and headed to my lonely oversized master bedroom to pull up his promised e-mail.

It was a long e-mail. He laid out all that he had been thinking about and going through in the last several months. He poured out his heart. He said he was sorry. And he told me that he wanted to fight for our marriage.

"This may not work," he wrote, "and we may divorce, but if we divorce I want to know that we tried hard and did everything we could. It seems evident that I've lost you, but if there's any hope, just call me after you read this and we can talk."

Reading his words, my heart exploded in my chest. All the dark and desperate moments of anxiety and stress and hurt drained away—replaced by a bright wide light of hope. I couldn't get to the phone fast enough. My hands were shaking as I dialed his number. He picked up.

"Hello?"

I took a deep breath and said, "Jeremy Lee, there is always hope."

And with that, Jeremy began to weep into the phone. He cried. I cried. And the silent spaces were filled with a sense of something new being created between us.

"I can't make any promises," Jeremy said. "I know this is going to take a long time. I know that you probably don't want me to move back in at least not yet, so I'm not going to move back in until you are ready. But I will do whatever it takes. I'm so sorry Tiffany. I'm just so, so sorry."

Sometimes hope comes in small doses just a little bit at a time. And then sometimes it rolls over us like a semitruck, flattening us with its abundance. In the moments after our phone call, a wide road opened up to us. We didn't know what the future held. We didn't know how to fix our marriage. We were both broken in so many ways, but that is how God gave us back to each other: Broken, wounded, and yet hopeful.

Through the next months, we started a new kind of marriage. One that was open and honest and fragile. We took our time. We went to counseling a lot. We prayed a lot. We laughed a lot. We cried a lot.

We started simply, by just hanging out as a family. No dating. No touching. Jeremy didn't move back into the guest room until months later. He held my hand for the first time on May 16, and we began dating again. We went to counseling religiously, and still do. We've learned that it's healthy and preventative to do so. It will forever be a priority with us.

In the process, we learned how to love each other again. It was baby steps, and we took our time. We wanted to get it right. Months after holding hands, we said, "I love you" for the first time since it had all begun, through tears of disbelief.

Months after that Jeremy offered me my wedding rings back and asked that I wear them. I had returned my rings to him many months before, saying I couldn't wear them with peace until he was the one asking me to wear them again.

And on Valentine's Day 2013, we got each other's initials tattooed on our ring fingers. It was our second matching tattoo; we had gotten the first ones shortly after we were newly married: *Yadah*, Hebrew for "to know," as in to know in the biblical sense, to be of one flesh. Both tattoos were symbols of permanence. Hope upon hope upon hope. And it just kept getting better.

# Chapter 22
## Hope & More Hope

IN THE LAST YEAR WHILE I have been on tour, Jeremy and I have made it a point to take the kids along. They need to be with me and I need to be with them. When I know Jeremy, Solomon, Oliver, and Clementine are flying to meet me somewhere on the road, I am so excited I can hardly stand it.

Sometimes during my set, the kids hang out and watch me from the sidelines. They have heard me mention several times from stage that a couple of years ago, Jeremy and I were teetering on the brink of divorce when God took off His gloves and told Satan where he could stick it. I always finish by saying there is always hope.

While at home recently, it came up in conversation.

"I don't know if you guys listen to what Mommy says before the show every night, but I love your daddy and your daddy loves me, and we will be married to each other until we're dead. But there was a time, when you were younger, when evil tried to tear our family apart."

They were listening closely so I wanted to give them an example they could understand.

"But God's so much greater than that. You know how Gandalf from the *Lord of the Rings* is so tall and so kind and so wise and so strong?"

"Yeah," they said in unison. (They are big *Lord of the Rings* fans.)

"Well, that's like God. And you know the little lizard on that car commercial?"

"Yeah."

"That's kind of like evil," I said, "weak, not able to do anything for you."

"Yeah!" The kids said.

"Well, there was a time when he was trying to convince Daddy and me that we shouldn't be married and that we should divorce each other. He wanted to break up our family, but we decided to choose to listen to God instead.

"You always have a choice. That is one of God's most precious gifts. God doesn't force you to choose Him. We are so thankful that an incredible community surrounded us and helped us to choose God's way, and God honored that choice and fought for us and He won. Just like Gandalf would win out over a lizard. Because of God's strength, because of hope, your daddy and I have a better marriage than we've ever had."

"Okay." (They were so cute listening so intently.)

"You're so young you probably don't understand all of this, and you may not even remember it all one day, but it's just part of who our family is now."

The kids sat quietly for a second and then someone asked, "Okay, so can we go to Dairy Queen tonight?"

To them my story was just one more chapter in Mom and Dad's story, a story they were important characters in. Mine was a chapter—not the end of the story. My friend Angie Smith had said basically the same thing over a long coffee earlier that winter, "Chapters are *part* of the story but don't have to be the end."

May 16, 2013, saw one of my favorite chapters unfold. It was one year from the day Jeremy Lee and I had held hands for first time since

149

our separation, marking our official start down the road to reconciliation. I knew that he was planning a special date for us to celebrate, because he had arranged for me to get my hair and makeup done as a treat. My hair and makeup stylist was unusually excited. She even had a bouquet of flowers for me. By the time I got home from the salon, Melis had already picked up the kids. I changed into a cute sundress.

Melis had earlier helped me set up a Spotify account as a gift for Jeremy. Couldn't have done it without her. She always knows who sings what, and technology is not my strong suit. I gave Jeremy my gift when we got in the car, and we began listening to the playlist I had put together for him. It was all of the songs I had listened to while we were separated and all the songs that had come to mean something to us since we reconciled. Jeremy began to cry, so I began to cry.

Wiping his eyes, Jeremy handed me a blindfold. *I do love surprises.* I put on the blindfold and didn't ask a single question. My heart was thumping. I had no idea what he was up to, and I'd decided I wasn't going to try and figure it out. I was too excited about the idea of a surprise. We drove for several minutes and then Jeremy stopped the car.

"Tif, I want you to keep your eyes on me when I take off the blindfold, okay?"

"Okay."

"Don't look around."

"Okay."

He removed the blindfold. "Do you know where we are?"

"We are at Centennial Park."

We were at the park where he had told me he loved me for the first time, the park where he had proposed to me one year later. And here we were, again. What took place next, I still pinch myself about.

"Will you marry me?" he asked. "All over again, will you marry me? Right now."

I couldn't help thinking it would have been more beautiful if he had asked me in the park instead of the car, but it sure didn't change my answer.

"Yes! Of course."

"Marry me right now," he said, grinning.

Having promised not to look around after Jeremy removed the blindfold, what I had failed to notice were our forty friends—the same forty friends who had held that prayer vigil for us when we separated so long ago—all seated in white rental chairs waiting to watch us marry all over again. They were present to watch us do what they had prayed for so diligently. They were present to watch God redeem only what He could redeem.

To say that I burst into tears would be a bit of an understatement. When I saw our friends sitting waiting for us, I buried my face in the blindfold (I am a terribly ugly crier). I wept so hard I couldn't catch my breath. My car door opened, and Melis grabbed me like I was back from the dead. Funny, when you think about it, given that a resurrection was what we were about to celebrate.

When I finally composed myself, the three most beautiful children I have ever laid eyes on crept around a tree, dressed in their best, eager to walk Mommy and Daddy down the aisle. Then I lost it on a whole new level.

Jeremy Lee walked me over to some lovely trees, on which several wedding dresses hung. I could hardly talk.

"Go ahead and pick one," he said.

A few of my girlfriends appeared with black sheets and fashioned an impromptu changing room for me. I chose the most beautiful dress I have ever seen, a floor-length ivory gown from one of my favorite stores, BCBGMAXAZRIA. It had thin stripes of black running down the front and back and three-quarter-length sleeves. It was breathtaking.

When I emerged from behind the sheets, there stood my handsome groom in a white dress shirt and light blue sports jacket holding purple hydrangeas.

Tulips and hydrangeas are my favorite flowers. Purple is my favorite color. Tara was videotaping everything just like she had when we got engaged years before. Justin, my keyboard player, played his accordion as we made our way down the aisle with Clementine, Solomon, and Oliver on either side of us.

Clementine was the flower girl and maid of honor. The boys were her escorts. When we reached the end of the aisle, our campus pastor, Justin Davis, and his wife, Trisha, were waiting for us. Justin had written vows for us and we read them. The cleansing tears that streamed down our cheeks seemed to heal every hurting spot from the past eighteen months.

We were new. We were better than before and more in love than I could ever have dreamed possible. We sealed our emotional vows with a kiss. You could feel the joy in the air.

Melis took pictures, and then we climbed in the car and headed to the small restaurant that Jeremy had rented out.

Dinner was waiting for us as was a beautiful wedding cake (no funky Eighties cake with weird pillars this time). Candles were lit and music played. Surrounded by our dearest friends, we ate, we drank, we caked, and we kissed. And then we headed to a beautiful hotel in Nashville for the night to honeymoon all over again. This time it was perfect—redemptive and pure.

We had come full circle, Jeremy Lee and I. We had married in 2000 but this new marriage promised to be better and stronger. It had survived chaos and hurt and loss, and then love showed up again. It had redeemed and healed and woven our hearts together in a new way, in ways we could never have imagined.

Our second wedding day is hands down the best day of my life so far. I was brimming over with love, and knew beyond a shadow of a doubt that I was loved in return.

I know there are many more wonderful days to come that Jeremy and I will have together. We have promised each other to stick together until we are old and gray.

You see, there is one irrefutable truth about us: I love Jeremy Lee. He loves me. We love Jesus. And we believe in resurrection.

Looking back over all the long years of dreaming, of wishing, of crazy circumstances, of babies, of heartache, of forgiveness and love beating out the odds, I am overwhelmed with God's love: With His grace. With His goodness. With His mercy. With His hope and with

His joy. Careers can change. Circumstances can change. People can change. But God was and is and is to come. No matter what. He is. And He is love. He is hope.

And as Jeremy and I look to the future, we know one more irrefutable truth that will hold us until eternity: There is always hope.

# Afterword

One of my favorite authors, Beth Moore, has said that God wants to take your pain and give it purpose. It's not that I hope that more bad things happen in my life but I can say that God took the most painful situation in my life and brought beauty out of it. He took chaos and brought order. He took pain and brought healing. He took hurt and brought peace. I have been completely in the dark and felt the bright light of hope warm me from the inside out. He can use our darkest deepest sorrow and our greatest hurts for good, too. He can bring beauty from the dark places in our lives if we let Him. He has done it for me. I know that He can do it for you.

One of my favorite quotes in the world is the one printed on the outside of the card that Breanna, my incredibly inspiring fan, handed to me the night I was considering ending Plumb. It reads:

> *The tender reed*
> *Bent to the force of the wind*
> *Soon stood upright once the storm had past.*

I have written this book with one thought in mind: Hope. Hope. Hope. We have all been bent by the force of the wind at one time or another in our lives. We have all felt beaten down, tossed aside, and forgotten. But that is not the end of the story. That dark place, that place where you feel like you have nowhere else to go or nowhere else to turn is the exact place where you can find that one drop of hope, the hope that can fill you up and straighten you up, tall and strong, even better than before, after the storm has passed.

Wherever you are, whoever you are, whatever you have done, whatever is happening in your life, please take this irrefutable truth for your own and tell yourself as often as necessary . . .

*There is always hope.*

Love,

Plumb

# For Marriages in Crisis

For those who might be facing a marriage crisis, here is a list that I made after the resurrection and restoration of our marriage. It's a list of the top things God used in our life to bring us back to Him. These are not laws, simply suggestions that worked for us.

### Counseling

If you don't know of a well-respected, licensed Christian marriage and family therapist in your area, go to a respected church leader and ask for a recommendation. If that isn't an option for you, you can go to *www.aacc.net* to find one locally. Please understand, this website lists any licensed Christian marriage and family therapist who wishes to be on it. It does not discriminate as to level of expertise. Do your research and get references. It's important for you to go to counseling both together and separately. But no matter what your spouse does, go.

### Community

Surround yourself with people who are for your marriage—and for you both. Not just for you or just for your spouse. Not people who have taken a side. Although well meaning, those persons can be divisive in your efforts to reconcile. A good sign that someone is on your side versus the side of your marriage is if they do things or make comments that make you feel defensive of your spouse. Allow your community to be brutally honest with you and hold you accountable so that you can do your part in owning what is yours and working on you. Ask them to listen, to help when you need it, and to pray often. Most importantly, give them permission to encourage you to seek the advice of your counselor in what you choose to do or say when it comes to your marriage, not them. Community can be a strength holding you up, a breath of fresh air when you feel like you're drowning, or a hand when you cannot stand on your own, but a licensed clinician is trained and educated specifically for your circumstance. Well meaning friends and family can be a toxic poison.

### Be honest with yourself

No matter what your spouse has said or done, what are the things you can change to make you more like the person God wants you to be? Spouse or no spouse, you will always benefit from being willing to do whatever it takes to be the healthiest you can be.

### Literature

Here are some of the priceless books we either read at different points in our crisis or that were invaluable to bringing us to where we are now.

*Sacred Marriage* by Gary Thomas
*The Meaning of Marriage* by Tim Keller
*Beyond Ordinary* by Justin and Trisha Davis
*Choose Joy* by Kay Warren
*Empty Promises* by Pete Wilson
*Let Hope In* by Pete Wilson
*Three Questions for a Frantic Family* by Patrick Lencioni
*James: Mercy Triumphs* by Beth Moore

### The Love Dare 40 Day Journal

This forty-day book/journal greatly influenced my desire to work on me, and without it I wouldn't have known where to start on some things—things I wasn't even aware that I did, things I didn't realize I needed to do but wasn't. It gives you forty dares (they can take much longer than forty days mind you) that change you. No matter what has happened in your marriage, the love dare is an incredible way to put a mirror up to your life and marriage and change the one thing for which you do have control: Your actions. Your responses. You.

### Protect the Innocent

One of the best pieces of advice our therapist ever gave us was that if there was even one shred of hope, even the tiniest of chances that we would stay married, to leave our children out of our conflict as much as possible. I am not suggesting that you lie to your children, however, I am saying that so much of a child's identity is found in his or her parents. Children's understanding of God is found in their mother and father until they are old enough to develop that personal relationship with Him. So keep your negative comments to yourself. And get creative with the truth in an effort to not project your fears and insecurities onto your children. If you love them, you want what is best for them. And what is best for them during a marriage crisis is to feel as loved and secure as possible. I realize certain things are unavoidable, but disclosing what Daddy said or Mommy did or making character judgments about someone they love so much will only hurt them, the innocent.

# Acknowledgments

Thanks to Sue Foth Aughtmon, who I already respected so much as one of my favorite rock star authors, and now it's my honor to call you friend. Thank you for helping to keep me focused (Lord knows I needed all the help I could get!) and for walking alongside me so closely to help navigate all of my stories that became this book.

To my manager, Chris Bradstreet, for your keen insight, your belief in my story, and your incredible vision for me to not just author books but this book specifically. Thank you for this challenge. For being unafraid to "lower the boom" with my hot mess and push me toward something I'm not sure I would have ever had the courage to do.

To some of my favorite authors who have helped to shape and inform my story: Kay Warren, Beth Moore, Patrick Lencioni, my incredible pastor Pete Wilson of Cross Point Church in Nashville, Angie Smith, mentors Justin and Trisha Davis, Gary Thomas, and Tim Keller, to name a few. Your wisdom has educated and empowered me to do this.

To Dr. Rebekah Land, whose wise counsel was the single most important ingredient God used in us being able to tell *this* story and not one of defeat. Jeremy Lee and I love and respect you so very much.

To my parents and my in-laws and all of my extended family, your support and belief in me means much more than you know. Our family dysfunction made my story more interesting and humorous to tell. Many of you fought for us as we came through our winter, and our relationship is stronger for it.

# Acknowledgments

To my assistant Miranda for keeping my calendar balanced and helping keep this on schedule. It wasn't easy!

To my incredible community of friends who have helped babysit or met for pizza so Jeremy and I could still have date nights and a "normal" life while I juggle wife, mom, touring artist, songwriter, and now author. There are too many of you to name, but please trust me that your selflessness has not gone unnoticed. I'm grateful.

Special thanks to friends Tara, Tammy, Leona, Ricky and Sami, Brent and Daveta, Dee, Dodge and Joy, Bryan, T.J., Megan and Nick, Chris and Laura, Phyllis, Sarah J., Lisa S., and Ann R. You still bear the scars of the battle you helped us to fight. We will never forget it. This is your story, too.

To Melis, for always being my C.C. Bloom. You are one of the leading roles in this story of hope. Thank you for telling me the truth and making me better. For getting down in the trenches and fighting for us, even if that meant you had to fight us. I love you, Kudus. You have been one of the biggest inspirations of my life. Your love and loyalty give me the courage to try. I would not be who I am today without you. I'm so excited for what is to come for you and T.J.

To Jeremy Lee, Solomon Fury, Oliver Canon, and Clementine Fire, for loving me so incredibly well and for the time you spent being patient while I wrote, skyped with Sue, visited with Sue, stayed up late writing, and made lame breakfasts because of my sleepy self. You will never know how much you mean to me but I will spend forever trying to show you. This is not *my* story, it is *our* story. And I am so honored to share it with you. I love you.

And to Jesus. It wasn't until You were truly all that I had that I found out You were all that I will ever need. Thank you for replacing so much of my fear with faith in Your protection, provision, and unconditional love. My cup overflows. I truly believe in resurrection now. Because of the cross . . . because of You, *There is always hope.* I love You with all that I am and all that I have. Use this book to glorify You.